To Sienna

Always believe in yourself!

"When you wish upon a Star your dreams come

Stefanie Jean Scott

"Philippians 4:13"

STARLITE MIST

A New Beginning

"Book One of the Starlite Mist Trilogy"

STEFANIE JEAN SCOTT

InspiringVoices®

Inspiring Voices books may be ordered through booksellers or by contacting:

Inspiring Voices
1663 Liberty Drive
Bloomington, IN 47403
www.inspiringvoices.com
1 (866) 697-5313

ISBN: 978-1-4624-0738-5 (sc)
ISBN: 978-1-4624-1256-3 (hc)
ISBN: 978-1-4624-0739-2 (e)

Library of Congress Control Number: 2013917462

Print information available on the last page.

Inspiring Voices rev. date: 05/13/2020

★ DEDICATION ★

I DEDICATE THIS BOOK to my miracle, my daughter, Crystal Jean. You are the one who encouraged me the most to finish this book and to share it with others, who love animals as much as we do. You are my greatest accomplishment. The doctor placed you in my arms on the day you were born, and my heart leaped. I couldn't believe God would bless me with such an amazing gift. I had prayed for you for such a long time. When I saw you for the very first time and held you on my chest, I was completely overcome with joy. I have never loved anything so much. It has been you and me, facing the world together your whole life, and I couldn't be more blessed. I am very proud of you!

If I could have written a letter to God and asked Him for everything I could have ever wanted in a child, the letter would have been a perfect description of you. You are strong and independent, and you are a hard worker. You are so creative. You are an amazing artist, and you have taught yourself to do so many creative things. I admire the way you draw, sew, and create pottery. I am so proud of you for having the courage to be the only girl in your Auto Body Tech Class and doing exceptionally well in it. I am so proud of you for taking your horse and going off to college over four hundred miles away to study horses.

I cannot tell you how proud of you I am for overcoming all that you endured and getting back on track. We had a super scary few years and you experienced a world no mother would ever want her child to see. It was by the grace of God that you survived it. I will never be anything but proud of you for overcoming it. I never knew someone could have so much courage, be so determined and could work so hard on herself. But you did and you were and you are! You are beyond amazing, Crystal Jean! None of any of that was in vain. God used you to save the lives of others and your story will save even more. You have a legacy to leave. You are truly an inspiration. I am nothing but proud of you, and so very grateful for your life! Lastly, I am proud of you for how you love. You take little babies into your heart and love them like they are your own. And through your loving them, I get to be one of their grandmas. That is pretty remarkable. Those babies have an auntie and a gram, because you chose to love them and their mommies. Not everyone can love like that. Not everyone chooses to love that way on purpose, so selflessly.

You have made me so proud over these past twenty-eight years. You have your own ideas, and even if I don't agree with all of them, I never want you to forget how proud of you I am. It takes courage, dedication, and hard work for you to accomplish your dreams. And Crystal Jean, it doesn't matter how many detours you may take or how long you may wander throughout this life. God is right beside you every single step of the way, and He will never leave you, not even for a second. Nothing you do could ever make me or God love you less. I pray you never, ever forget where you came from. I pray you will always remember the day you were saved, the moment you were baptized, and every single experience you ever had with Jesus. I pray that you will cherish all the ones that are to follow. He has so much to show you.

Please remember that every human heart has a God-shaped hole in it, that only God can fill. When you find yourself searching for someone or something to fill it, I hope you will remember He is right there, waiting to fill it for you. He wants a relationship with you. He loves you so much, more than anyone ever can. He wants you to know you are a masterpiece. You are amazing. You are enough. And you are *His*. He created you, and He wants you to fall in love with Him again. And remember, God has no grandchildren. You are His daughter. You alone must answer to your heavenly Father. You are the only one responsible for the choices you make. Please don't ever forget these things, honey. They are truth. They are life. They are everything. I love you to the moon, around every single planet, through the Milky Way, and back. I will love you for always and forever, and no matter what. Don't ever forget that, my red-haired, horse-crazed Mini Me. I love ya ta peaches, Crystal Jean! Love, Yo Mama.

I also dedicate this book to the little ones who made me a Gram, because of my daughter's precious heart: Raelyn, our Little Rae of Sunshine, my gorgeous little granddaughter, you were the first to make me a gram. Oh how you resemble Crystal when she was your age.

I so love the fun we have together. I love teaching you to ride Dusty, you are a natural. I love our scooter rides and taking you to church with the ragtop down in the Mustang. I love our daytrips to parks, splash pads, the pool and the lake. You are so fun and adventurous and funny and perfect. I just love being your Gwam. Thank you, Liesl, for letting me be your baby's Gwam. You are such a wonderful Mama. I am so lucky to have you as my 'other daughter.' I love you, Honey!

Next to call me Gram is Tabor Joseph, oh mylanta! What can I even say? You have been a whirlwind of awesome since the day you were born. There has never been a dull moment in any of our lives, since God blessed us with you. I cannot believe how smart you are. You are just so articulate, artistic and amazing. You are so fun and outgoing and full of life! You love to swim, you make the most incredible LEGO creations and your drawing skills are off da chain! You get amazing grades, mostly A's and you are doing very well in Taekwondo. You have been riding Dusty since you were *four* and you too are a natural. I don't know anyone else who would zip line with me, especially at the young age of just barely *six*! I can't get over how completely fearless and intentionally courageous you are. You are totally the coolest kid I know. I am so lucky to be raising you. I just love being your Ga'am *and* your Mommy.

Then there is our sweet baby Roman, what a precious miracle you are. From the moment that you were conceived you were a blessing. I loved being the one to give you your first bath up in the hospital. I cherish every memory we made. You will always be our heaven sent blessing and you will always be loved by us.

Next there is my oldest grandson, Eli. You are so sweet and smart and strong. From scouts to piano, robotics to cello (and many other instruments), baseball to outstanding grades in school, and the list goes on; wow, how you amaze me! You are growing up to be an amazing young man. I am so very blessed to be your Grams. Thank you Amy and Jay, for adopting me as your son's Grams. I love you two!

I dedicate this book also to: Mackinzie, our precious little angel baby. Meeting you the day you were born and having to say goodbye all at the same time was more than any of us could stand. You were so perfect and beautiful and so very sweet. I look forward to the day when I can hold you in my arms, you and your beautiful momma, too. You are both loved and missed and cherished, oh so very much.

Next, Lizzie M., who is my little 13 going on 30 year old. With every strong-willed decision you make, I truly believe that your determination will someday guide you into an even stronger leadership role. I am so proud of you. You are bold and brave and beautiful, inside and out. I dedicate this book to your two oldest siblings as well.

Then there is Lizzy L., who is our talented little musician, and the one girl that everyone wants on their team. I love how you can just pick up learning music and be so good at it, in no time. You are such an amazing young lady. I love our talks and how sweet you always are. You are so beautiful and I just adore you.

Next is Jasmine, my adorable, sweet, kind, awesome, beautiful girl. I love, love, love, love our chats. And I love when you surprise me with a text out of nowhere. You brighten my day and put a smile on my face, every time! Robert "Bobby" and Leann, thank you for giving me the honor of being your babies' Nanny, and for loving me like your own "extra" mom. I am so blessed to have you in my life. You are doing an amazing job raising your children and loving each other. Through every battle and every victory, I am in your corner cheering you on every step of the way! I love you and your children so very much.

I want to also dedicate this book to: Mia and your baby sibling who is due to be born this year! Mia…oh my, oh my, oh my! I don't think that I have *ever* seen such an adorable little cutie pie like you, ever before in my life! You stole my heart the moment we met. You are so happy and so full of character and so, oh my goodness, adorable! I am so excited that you are going to be a big sister this year! You are going to be the best big sister ever! We love you!

I dedicate this book also, to Michael, the one little baby boy that I cherished oh so much, worried forever about as a little one, and was blessed beyond belief at the amazing young man that you have grown up to be. Next, is Blake, our little muscle man, so tough and strong and cute. I can't believe how grown up you are now. I will never forget the day you were born. I didn't want to put you down. I could have held you forever. And then there is our beautiful Meadow. You were our first Little Princess, and oh my goodness, how you held that title with honor! What can I say? You have been such a precious little blessing since day one. Katrina and Steve, you did so good, raising these three so well and standing by each other through this crazy ride called life. I am so very proud of you two.

Thank you for all of the memories that we made. I love you all! Though the miles may separate us, and even though our communication is not constant, I think of you always and pray for you daily. You each hold a very special place in my heart. All of you have such amazing qualities and gifts, and I am so proud of the people that you are growing up to be. I thank God that you are in my life and I love you all ta peaches!

I also dedicate this book to Colin, and Bailee. You have blessed me beyond words. It is a privilege to have been a part of your childhood. It is an honor to love you. I am so proud of the amazing people that you have grown up to be. I will always love you.

In addition, I dedicate this book to my amazing nephew, Chris Jr., and your beautiful wife, Kali and your three adorable, smart, funny, precious children: Saphira, Phoenix and Melody. Chris, I am so very, very proud of you! I am proud of the honorable work that you do for our country, and I am so proud of you and Kali for doing such a great job raising your sweet children. I cannot praise you two enough! I love you all so much.

I dedicate this book also, to my awesome nephew Timmy. You just graduated high school and I am so very proud of you! Way to go! You did it! I am looking forward to cheering you on in the next chapter of your life. I love you! I dedicate this book to my other wonderful nephews: Anthony and Thomas. I am so proud of the men that you have grown up to be. You are both hard workers and such great people. I will never forget the day you both asked Jesus into your hearts. I dedicate this book to my beautiful niece, Kimberly, your husband, Titus and your two precious, smart, adorable little boys, my great nephews: Tate and Toby. I am so very proud of each of you; for the amazing people that you are, the way you choose to love Jesus and others, all of the accomplishments that you keep surprising me with. The list is endless, and so is my love for you.

In addition, I dedicate this book to Darlene and my babysitters; Lillian (and your sisters and mom), Cheryl and Kaleb and my good friends Lisa C. and Lisa S. Thank you for all of your help with my little boy.

I would like to also dedicate this book to my three precious Godchildren: Princess Payton Marie, our firstborn and only baby girl, so far. You are so smart and so loving and such a good big sister to your baby brothers. We are all amazed at how grown up you are at the very young age of three. Roi Kevin, our first prince, who is either concentrating on a good movie or just being a wonderful brother. You are brilliant and awesome and you are just one amazing little man! Princton Mal'akhi, our second prince and also our baby. I remember the day you were born as I held you up in the hospital doting over you. You are so precious and adorable and oh so feisty! You are such an awesome little guy. I adore you three so much. I am so very blessed to be your Godmommy. I just love you three ta peaches! Thank you so much, Tori for giving me the opportunity to be in your lives. You are one of the best little mommas I know and I am so very proud of you!

In addition, I dedicate this book to all of my patients and their families; especially Kayden, Jenny and Benji. I also dedicate this book to my fellow foster families. I had no idea that God would bring me to becoming a foster mom, but here I am! I am so grateful for all of the training, love, support, and new friendships that I now have. And lastly, I dedicate this book to "Team Tabor" all of the amazing men and women who have helped me advocate for my little man. Thank you for your guidance and training and encouragement! I couldn't have done any of this without you. It truly does take a village to do what we do. I love you all so much and I am so thankful for all of you.

★ SPECIAL DEDICATION ★

I DEDICATE THIS BOOK especially to my wonderful pony, Starlite Mist. You were my dream come true, the desire of my heart, my little dumpling. Thank you for learning to trust me and for loving me back. You never gave up on you. Through all your training and the tough love that went into it, you always trusted me. You must have known it was necessary to save your life. And in so doing, you saved mine in many, many ways. God placed you in my life at just the right moment. You were there through all my tough teenage years at the scary time of transitioning from a child into a teenager. You were with me as I grew from a teenager into a woman, and you were there for me at my most wonderful times, when I became a bride and a mommy.

You and I have traveled some rough roads together, Starsy. Through all the pain you went through to make you live again, you toughed it out. You showed the world who you really were, a precious miracle, beautiful both inside and out. God gave you a chance to live again, and you took it. At the same time, He showed me how to truly live too. He taught me how to love unconditionally, how to forgive others, and how to trust Him. I am so proud of you, my Starsy! You are such a big part of me. I thank God for you. I will always love you, *always*!

Love, your Steffer

★ TABLE OF CONTENTS ★

★ ACKNOWLEDGMENTS ★

I WOULD LIKE TO first thank Jesus, my Savior and my very Best Friend. Thank You for loving me. Thank You for saving me. Thank You for giving me a love for horses. And thank You for giving me this story to tell. This book was written for You, Lord. May this story give You glory! My faith in You gave me the hope, dedication, and drive to accomplish every goal that was set before me. You made me wait until I was ready, and then You gave me the desire of my heart. Thank You for my Starsy. She forever changed my life. I love You, Jesus!

I would also like to thank my loving parents, Tim and Sharon Hacker. Dad, your love for animals was passed down to me, and I am so grateful for that. You understood firsthand how much I loved my pets while growing up, and you allowed me to have all the pets I ever asked for. You made sure you taught me how to care for all of them with gentleness and tenderness. You were and still are the coolest dad around. I love you more! I love you most! I love you more than all the stars in the sky. And I love you more than I ever knew. I hope I have made you proud.

Dad, I know we don't see eye to eye on everything, and our debates can get pretty touchy. But I get that strong sense of opinion from you, and I thank you for it. I always look forward to coming over and watching our favorite shows together. I wouldn't trade our bond for anything. You taught me to work hard, to never sell myself short, and to never sell out. You raised me with values and a strong sense of self-respect. You always made sure you gave me hope. And you *always* made sure you taught me and my sisters about God, Jesus, and the Holy Spirit. You were adamant about making sure we knew Him and continued to learn about Him.

If we had questions you couldn't answer, you took us to pastors, churches, and even seminars to find those answers. Only an awesome dad does that. Nothing you ever did for us was in vain. We all love

God. We all go to church. And we will all spend eternity in heaven together, because of you. You chose to love God and to accept His gift of salvation through Jesus Christ, and then you led us there too. Thank you, Dad, for being there for me through this crazy ride called life. I know I put you through a *lot*, and I am so grateful you went through it all with me. You didn't have to. I am so blessed to have you as my dad. I couldn't imagine my life without you. Thank you for *everything*!

Mom, I wanted to have this first book completed before you went home to be with Jesus, but that didn't happen. As it turned out, that gave me more time with you, and I wouldn't have wanted it any other way. With every pot of coffee we shared, we made a memory. I don't know of a mother who ever loved like you did ... except for your own mom and sisters. What a blessed kid I was. What a blessed woman I am. Most people *might* be fortunate to meet a woman like you *once* in their lifetime. I was lucky enough to be *raised* by you. I thank God for that all the time. Thank you for loving me unconditionally, Mom. Thank you for believing in me and supporting me in every crazy adventure I found myself in. Thank you for always making me feel loved, wanted, and important. Even in the smallest achievements, you praised me and made me feel like I could do anything. You were my cheerleader, my mentor, my shoulder to cry on. You gave me hope, encouragement, and confidence. You told me I could become anything I wanted to be. Your dream was to see me finish college, and so I did. Because of you, I am a Pediatric Home Care Nurse. If I can be half the woman you were, I will be so grateful. You were and still are the most precious person I have ever known. I miss you every minute. I thank God you were born again, and I know you are in heaven. I take comfort in knowing that one day we will meet again on that beautiful shore. Mom, when I want to see your face, when I just cannot stand that you are so far away, I remember that you can be found in Proverbs 31. Thank you for being the best role model a girl could have. You were the best mama ever!

I would also like to thank my amazing sisters, Sandy and Cindy. I was born 5 and 6 years after you and you two looked after me our entire childhood. I was your living baby doll and you both loved me with your whole hearts. You played with me, babysat me, tutored me, protected me from bullies, and drove me and my friends anywhere we wanted to go. You took me to church. You taught me the facts of life. I could count on both of you for anything. You were and still are my very best friends. I cannot thank you both enough for all you have done for me throughout our lifetime. When God placed Star and I together, you never hesitated to help us. You both took so much time out of your busy schedules day after day, month after month, year after year to drive me back and forth to and from the barn. There was no way I could have rehabilitated my pony without you two. Thank you for being the best big sisters a girl could ever have. And thank you to my super cool brother-in-law Chris, for being such a great husband to my sister Cindy and such a wonderful father to my nephews; but mostly, thank you for loving Jesus.

I want to give a great big thank-you to Missy for giving me my pony, Star. Without you, I never would have had this story to share with others. Your gift was priceless. I know I wouldn't be the person I am today without her having been in my life. That little pony went on to touch the lives of other children and adults as well. She was a Godsend to many. Our paths crossing over thirty years ago wasn't a coincidence; it was a "God"-incidence. May God give back to you all the happiness you have given to me and more. I pray He will wrap you up tight in His arms of love and that He will give you comfort and peace and hope like you have never known. May He fill you up with so much joy that you can hardly stand it. I pray that God will remind you often of the fact that He created you and that you are amazing, you are enough, and you are *His*.

Thank you Chuck (Missy's dad), for raising such a wonderful daughter, introducing us and making all this happen. And thank you for being such a great friend to my dad.

In addition, I want to thank my childhood friends: my best friend, Cheryl, who stood by me every step of the way. From teenagers to adults, from best friendship to photography, from computer technology to proofreading, you have helped me with every need regarding this book. Cheryl, I "cher"-ish our friendship. I love you, Chew!

I also want to give thanks to Darnelle for keeping the love of horses deep within my spirit no matter how much we fought with each other, which was pretty often.

I would like to thank Stephanie (Bucky) for being such a blessing in my life. God brought us together when we were in diapers, and now He brought us back together as adults. I thank Him for that pretty often.

I would like to thank Jessica for being there for me during our entire childhood. I will never forget when God brought us together on our first day of preschool.

I would like to thank my cousin Brad for growing up with me and putting up with me my entire life. Brad, you have always been more like a brother to me. I am glad our dads were best friends and we and our siblings were raised together. I am so thankful for you, your wife, Michelle, and your family: Zoe, Ellie, Wyatt and Sage, your parents J.C. and Janice, and your siblings Theresa, Brent and Lisa. My daughter, my little boy, and I are so blessed to have you all in our lives. You are a wonderful person and a great friend. Thanks for everything, Brubs.

There are so many other wonderful friends, too many to list, who also were there for me. But you know who you are. Thank you! I want to give thanks to my childhood horse and pony club; and to my county fair buddy, Miranda, who was only eight years old when she helped me with my pony every day at the fair. You were the little sister I never had.

A *big* thanks goes out to the owners and staff at Al-Bar Ranch Tack Shop in Mishawaka, Indiana. You were always so helpful in assisting me with all my equine needs, and you did the same twenty years later when my daughter was in fair. You were and still are the best tack shop around.

Thanks also to Jenna, another little girl who was very dear to me. You will hear more about her in the sequels to follow.

I also would like to thank Doc Marty for being the best vet my pony could ever have. You have been my mentor from Veterinary Science Club as a teenager to this present day, as an adult. You and your beautiful wife have touched the lives of countless children and adults alike, not to mention all of the animals that you have cared for. Thank you for helping me to see Jesus in everything I do.

I want to give special thanks to my very best friends and sisters in Christ: Dawn and Carrie. Thank you for helping me get this book together, for being there for me for over thirty years, for providing all your prayers and words of encouragement, and for loving Jesus like you do. Women who love God as much as you two do don't come along very often in a person's lifetime. I was blessed to have *both* of you for almost my entire life. I thank God for you, and I really don't know where I'd be without you both.

I want to thank Carey for being there for me as my friend, brother in Christ and fellow prayer warrior. You have blessed me in so many ways. Thank you for loving Jesus.

I want to thank my cousin Jason, who loves horses every bit as much as I do. And my cousin-in-law Ami, who helped shape me into the horsewoman I am today. Thank you to my cousin Larry who put up with me while I took up so much of your wife's time. I also want to thank my cousins Monika, Lori, and Leslie (and their siblings), who shared me with them during my summers in the beautiful state of Pennsylvania. I would also like to thank all my many cousins from Pennsylvania to California, the Philippines, Tennessee, Michigan, Illinois and Indiana. I love you all so very much!

A big thank you goes out to Roy "Cowboy" and his daughter, Debbie. You two helped me so much with my journey rehabilitating Star. From hauling her and I to the fair year after year, to loaning me show tack and always having our backs in various situations; you both deserve medals for all you have done for us. Your expertise, advice and guidance were such a treasure to us. You helped us more than you will ever know. You are good people and my dad and I are ever so grateful for your friendship.

I give another great big thank-you to the most amazing horseman I have ever known, Parry. Thank you for taking the time to make a little girl's dream come true. Thank you for giving an unfortunate pony a second chance at life and for helping me put all her missing pieces back together again. You believed in us. You were Star's angel. You are my hero. Thank you, thank you, *thank you*!

I would like to thank my precious grandparents for being the best grandparents a kid could ask for. I love you, Mama Jo- Josephine,

Gram-Blanche, Pappy-William I, Daddy Paw-Walter I, Grandpa Wayne, Grandma Ruth, Grandpa Curt and Grandma Mary. I want to thank all my loving aunts and uncles: Uncle Lou (Helen) (Jean), Uncle Bill (Dixie), Aunt Rosalie (Bob) (Gene), Aunt Charmaine (Ivan), Aunt Peggy (Larry), Aunt Dianna (Butch), Aunt Debbie (Mike), Uncle Jim (Margaret), and Aunt Betty Lou (Carl). I love you all!

Finally, I would like to thank my amazing pastor, Pastor Mark Beeson and his wonderful wife, "Ms. Sheila" Beeson. You two love Jesus so much, and your obedience to Him has brought countless souls into the Kingdom of Heaven. Your 33 years of ministry to our community and our world is completely astonishing. You lead by example, and what remarkable examples you both are. Your stories give Him glory. I could never thank you enough for all you have taught me.

As a teenager, 32 years ago, I went to see a movie and stumbled across your church, inside of a movie theater. There was no movie playing that day, but I stayed and watched a loving husband and wife teach people about the love of God. Years later, the church building was built just down the road from where that movie theater once stood. It is called Granger Community Church "GCC" and it is a bit different. It is now a mega-church where thousands come to worship every weekend. It has an amazing student ministry and the lower level children's ministry is the coolest thing I have ever seen! There are literally tube slides on the first level that the kiddos take down into their classrooms-what!? I took one tour of the children's ministry and thought, "Any Bible teaching church that puts THIS much effort into their children, is where I want to worship!"

I now bring my children, grandchildren, dad, cousins, friends, neighbors, and all the many little ones that I babysit, to GCC to learn about God's love. It has been a little over 13 years since I have been back in Indiana, and attending Granger Community Church, and every week I am completely beside myself in awe of how the Holy Spirit moves through your ministry. If I ever have to miss a service, for whatever reason, I am scrambling to my computer to watch it online. I don't want to miss a thing. It is just *that* good!

Thank you for caring so much about people. Thank you for helping us take our next steps toward Christ…together. Thank you for showing us that we each play a vital role in His story and for reminding us that we are irreplaceable, treasured and loved fiercely and intentionally by God Himself; and that He knows us each by name. Pastor Mark, Ms. Sheila, you remind us that if there were only one person to ever be created, Jesus would have still came to earth and died for that one. That is love and that is what you have taught us. Thank you! Thank you! Thank you! May God bless you both and your beautiful family, too.

★ THANK YOU! ★

I WOULD ALSO LIKE to give thanks to *you*. Thank you for taking the time to read this story. May it give you hope when you find you are running out. May it offer you encouragement when you need it the most, and may it remind you that you "can do *all* things through Christ who gives [you] strength!" (Philippians 4:13 NKJV, emphasis added). Remember, you are not here by chance. You were put on this earth on purpose for a purpose. God created you with His own hands, and you are a masterpiece. You are precious. You were created exactly the way God designed you to be. God says in His Word that you are "fearfully and wonderfully made" (Psalm 139:14 NKJV). He says "But the very hairs of your head are all numbered" (Matthew 10:29–31NKJV), you "were made in [My] own image" (Genesis 1:27 NKJV), and I "knit [you] together in [your] mother's womb" (Psalm 139:13 ESV). Everything you are—the way you look, the things you enjoy doing, the way you laugh—all those things are the way God created you to be. God says, "Before I formed you in the womb, I knew you… (Jeremiah 1:4–5 NKJV). He tells us in His Word that you are not a mistake. "And in Your book they all were written, the days fashioned for me…" (Psalm 139:15–16 NKJV). You are God's "…treasured possession…" (Exodus19:5 ESV). There isn't another person in the entire world that is exactly like you. You are one of a kind. You are an original design. God's love for you is incredible. You are awesome. And you are His. Please don't *ever* forget that:

"No matter what, you matter!"—Stefanie Jean Scott.

Note: Some names have been changed to protect privacy; however, this story is true, and it was written to give God glory.

★ INTRODUCTION ★

HAVE YOU EVER wanted something so badly that part of you ached inside, knowing it was out there somewhere, waiting for you to find it? Have you ever had a burning desire so intense that you worked and strived for years to obtain it? If you answered yes to these questions, then you know how a little girl named Steffy felt after discovering she had a very special gift, a love for horses.

In the pages of this book, you will discover the beauty of this incredible love. This is the true story of a little girl who went to great lengths to earn a horse of her very own, only to discover that the one thing she wanted more than anything else in the entire world needed her even more.

★ CHAPTER 1 ★

❧ *Wish upon a Star* ❧

T HE WARM SUN beat down on Steffy's round, freckled face as she looked up into the cloudless morning sky. From the feedback she had received at school, just about every child who had heard of Steffy's Diner planned on being there. No kid they knew had ever opened a diner before, and "for pennies, they could enjoy good food and hang out with their friends." Excitedly, Steffy examined the sign on the front porch door, making sure it was straight. Then she ran back inside the diner, a.k.a. the Hacker's front porch. The young girl raced around the porch, checking the list in her head.

"The tables from the playroom are washed and the chairs are pushed in," she said to herself. The miniature entrepreneur straightened up the napkins and made sure the floor was swept. Then she verified that the other furniture was right where it belonged. The coffee table and the end tables from the living room were in the corner of the diner, with the lawn chairs neatly pushed in under them. Then she made sure the barstools from the kitchen and the footrest from the living room were arranged to her liking. They were up against the wall of the porch, lengthwise for extra seating. She had them arranged just so, in case she got the response she was hoping for: countless customers.

The determined eight-year-old walked through the front door and into the living room. She was careful as she pushed open the window leading to the front porch. After that she placed a small box filled with change, which she had begged her sisters for, on the windowsill. She smiled with anticipation as she imagined that little cardboard box as a genuine cash register, like the kind used at supermarkets or department stores. With a look of satisfaction on her face, the little businesswoman inspected a pencil, holding its tip up to the sunlight. "Yep, it's sharpened," she said to herself. She neatly placed the pencil on the notebook next to her "cash register," ready to take her customers' orders.

Making her way into the kitchen, the little girl's eyes lit up, and a huge smile came across her slightly chubby face. There stood her two loyal sisters, also wearing smiles, ready for kitchen duty. The oldest at a sophisticated fourteen years, Sandy Jo, stood staring at Steffy with a look of admiration. Sandy had silky, light-brown, waist-long hair, which matched her sparkling light-brown eyes. She was a devout born-again Christian, who was always willing to lend Steffy a helping hand. She was also always happy to share her faith with everyone she met.

Cindy Lee, the middle sister, at a frisky thirteen years, looked at Steffy just as proud as can be, with a "LET'S DO THIS!" attitude. Cindy had thick, shoulder-length, dark-brown hair, which matched her beautiful yet curious dark-brown eyes. She also was devoted to her little sister. Cindy was always there to help Steffy with her wild ideas. However, she couldn't help but wonder what Mom and Dad were going to do to her little sister when they found out what she had been up to. Both of them had prepared the kitchen. Every item on the menu was ready to be whipped up by the ambitious teens in a matter of minutes. The girls had their brown hair pulled back in ponytails and their hands washed. They stood, eagerly awaiting their food orders.

"Great!" Steffy said. "It's almost eight o'clock. We should be getting our first customers soon. I'll be up at the window. Thanks, guys. You're the best!" Then one by one the neighborhood children piled into Steffy's Diner. The excited second-grader smiled from ear to ear as she took order after order. She ran back into the kitchen. "I need two pieces of toast, both buttered, please," she said.

Sandy quickly opened a bag of bread, pulled two pieces out, and put them in the toaster. Smiling, she pushed the button down into the on position.

"I need one with strawberry jelly and one with grape jelly," Steffy continued.

Cindy reached into the refrigerator and pulled out both jars of jelly, along with the butter.

"Okay, now I need two hot chocolates," Steffy added as she rushed back to the open window. *Wow!* There were a lot more kids coming than she had imagined. One by one, two by two, Steffy couldn't keep up the count. All the children seemed to be happy with the taste and the price of their food. In addition, they had the opportunity to hang out with each other without having to be in school. This was a pretty big deal in the 1970s! Back then there was no Internet, no cyber social networks, and certainly no such thing as a cell phone. Getting to hang out with friends in a kid-themed diner at their age was quite an awesome experience.

Everything on the menu was under a dollar. A slice of toast sold for ten cents. Add butter for a penny, and add jelly for a nickel. Hot chocolate sold for a dime. Add marshmallows for five cents more. A bologna sandwich sold for a quarter; add mayo for a penny (and so forth). The hours seemed to fly by, and the cash register filled up quickly. But then, just as quickly as the children arrived, they scattered when they heard Sandy yell, "Dad's home, everyone, leave!"

In no time flat, Steffy's Diner was completely empty. Cindy, being the clean freak, quickly began wiping off the countertops. She looked somewhat concerned as she put what little food they had left back in its place. Then she began filling the kitchen sink with dish water. Meanwhile, Sandy shot into the front porch like a bullet, helping Steffy put all the living room furniture back in its place. Then she ran back into the kitchen and started washing the dishes.

Steffy began sweeping the floor. Her heart began to beat fast as her dad made his way into the driveway and parked his old green van. Without knowing it, he bought his daughters some time. First, he fed his beloved pigeons. Then he greeted the family's three dogs and pet cat. Steffy's dad was an animal lover too. Their family always seemed to have as many animals as the city permitted. Currently, they had a beagle mix, a German shepherd mix, a Scottish terrier mix, and a tabby cat. All four animals were very loyal, and they were more like hairy siblings to the three sisters than pets.

As Steffy cleaned up her "job site," she thought about how hard her parents worked. It was common for both of them to work on the weekends. A strong work ethic ran through their blood, and

Steffy admired them for that. Her dad, Tim, worked long hours at an automobile factory, making city buses. Her mom, Sharon, worked in a factory making plastic parts for vehicles and machinery. While they were at work on that particular Saturday, it had seemed to Steffy that it might be a good time for her to make some money of her own. After all, that horse she was dreaming of wasn't gonna buy itself.

But now that her father was making his way through the back door and up the hallway steps, this little girl was having second thoughts. In fact, even though the house was clean and in order, she couldn't help but feel concerned. Was there a chance she could get in trouble for having Steffy's Diner? Or would her dad share her vision and be proud of her work ethic? Ready or not, she was about to find out.

As soon as he made eye contact with his three daughters, he could sense a bit of tension in the air. He decided his daughters may have been up to something. Then he received his hugs from each of his precious children. The last hug, from Steffy, was extra long and even included a peck on his scruffy cheek.

Yep, they are up to something all right, he thought.

Their dad was a unique guy. He wore his hair in a Fonzie/Elvis 1950's style, and the sleeves of his shirts had been cut off, exposing the muscles in his arms. He had charming blue eyes and a fit figure because he ate healthy, took plenty of vitamins, and lifted weights every day. All in all, he was a pretty good guy, and he was quite clever too.

So it didn't take long before his eyes became fixed on the living room window, which happened to be open with a box of money sitting on the windowsill. In deep thought, he headed toward the refrigerator. Then he opened the door and reached for a cold cola. Looking puzzled, he wondered where in the world all the food had gone. His next stop was the pantry. You can imagine his surprise when he saw it was only partially supplied with food. In addition, you can guess how bad Steffy felt as she saw the look of disappointment on her dad's face. Her worst fear was disappointing her parents.

You see, the day before had been payday for both of her parents, and her mom had just filled the fridge and the pantry with food. So the silence was deafening. You could have heard a pin drop. Steffy tried hard to swallow the lump now stuck in the back of her throat. Both of her sisters stood there, trying to think of excuses to leave the scene. Sandy suddenly remembered she had a very important homework assignment that needed her immediate attention. Then Cindy excused herself so she could polish her speed skates for the "All Night Skate" at the local roller rink that evening, leaving their little sister alone to explain the mystery of the "incredible vanishing groceries."

Steffy began explaining to her dad that she had opened a diner on their front porch earlier that day. She told him it had been a fund-raiser and that she actually had quite a good turnout. She also showed her dad the money she had made and proceeded to point out that all the children had had a great time. However, just as she had feared, her dad didn't seem to see her perspective, and being proud of her work ethic was the furthest thing from his mind.

As he scolded her for selling most of their family's groceries in one morning, Steffy felt like crying. She was so upset with herself. *Why didn't I think this idea through?* she thought to herself. All she had seen at the time were dollar signs and money. And money was what it would take to make her dream come true. For as long as she could remember, more than anything else in the entire world, Steffy had had a burning desire to have a horse of her very own. She had always loved wearing cowgirl boots and dressing up like a cowgirl. In fact, her favorite song in the whole wide world was "Rhinestone Cowboy." In addition, her favorite television show ever was *The Lone Ranger*.

Her passion for animals in general was pretty incredible. Steffy's entire eight years of life included caring for no less than three dogs and a cat. There had always been pigeons to care for too and some kind of pet rodent she'd managed to talk her parents into letting her have, be it gerbils, guinea pigs, hamsters, or domestic mice. One time she'd tried to raise a dozen toads she had caught in a creek, but that didn't go over too well. She had to take them back to the creek before they all died. She had no idea how to care for them. Back then there was no such thing as hopping on the internet (no pun intended) and Googling information; for computers were still a thing of the future. At one point, she even had a pair of turtles. She'd obtained those from a nearby pet store. She'd been able to speak to the pet store owner and learn how to care for them without a problem.

The little animal lover decided that having a horse of her very own would complete her as a pet owner. Her confirmation came when a little six-year-old girl named Darnelle moved in next door. Darnelle had come straight from horse country, and she and her parents had moved two houses down from Steffy and her family. The girls bonded instantly and became good friends. Darnelle told Steffy all about her very first ponies. Steffy fell in love with her new friend's stories, and she longed even more to have a horse of her own. At the age of eight, the love of horses began to flow red hot through her veins. It was in her blood, and there was no turning back. If you or someone you know ever acquires this gift or curse, however one may look at it, there really is no satisfying the craving. That person simply must somehow, some way, have a horse in their life. They will find a way to borrow, exercise, train, critter-sit or care for one in some way. Once a person has the horse lover's bug, he/she will never, ever be free of it. That person will love horses and need them until the day he/she leaves this earth.

Steffy was completely convinced she needed to have a horse of her own. But now with her dad scolding her like he was, she felt like a failure. He told her all the money she'd made from her sales at Steffy's Diner would have to go back into her family's grocery fund. The eight-year-old's little heart was crushed. How would she ever be able to buy a horse now? Her dad was very unhappy with her, *and* she had no money now. All the work she and her sisters had done that day had been for nothing. She felt as though her chances of ever getting a horse of her own were next to none.

As her dad's scolding continued, her mom arrived home from work. Despite the fact that she had just put in a full day of overtime, her mom, Sharon, glowed with beauty from the inside out. Her waist-long, golden-brown hair sparkled in the sunlight beaming through the kitchen window. She stood slim and fit in her blue jeans and light-blue cotton blouse. Her golden-brown eyes matched her sparkling hair.

Steffy's dad couldn't help but pause and stare at her as she entered the room. Steffy's mom was her hero, her role model, her mentor. She was smart and friendly, kind and caring. She was as beautiful on the inside as she was on the outside. Babies loved her, children adored her, and grown-ups wanted to be like her. Steffy knew having her for a mom was truly a blessing. Her mom's presence seemed to thin the tension in the air, which had been quite thick, and Steffy could breathe a little easier now.

Wondering what their daughter could have possibly done to deserve such a scolding, her mom listened carefully. Then her dad began to explain the details of her crime. After he had finished, her mom smiled a sympathetic smile and walked over to her sad little girl. Putting her arms around Steffy, she kissed the top of her head twice.

Feeling somewhat better, Steffy began to explain why she wanted to earn the money. "I want to save up money to buy a horse of my very own. I want to earn the money myself so you can be proud of me."

Her parents listened as she went on and on about how she felt she needed to have a horse. She tried desperately to tell them it wasn't just something she wanted but something she felt she *needed*. Their daughter went on to say many children want a horse or pony at some point in their lives, but then they outgrow it. Steffy explained how she felt, that she was different from those children. She just couldn't see herself growing out of this I-am-crazy-about-horses phase. It was important for her to help her parents understand, but she was afraid they wouldn't be able to see her point of view.

After they heard their daughter's plea, they told her that having a horse of her own was a very big responsibility. They helped her to understand that she needed their permission to have one. Then they told her that to have a business like Steffy's Diner on their front porch and to sell the family's groceries also needed to have their approval. Lastly, her parents made themselves very clear that, at the age of eight, she needed to earn a horse in a different way. Her parents said they would have to sit down and discuss the matter. Then they would get back to her and tell her how she could go about getting this horse she thought she needed so badly. So that was exactly what her parents did.

Steffy went to her room, cleaned it up, and made her bed, just in case having a clean bedroom would be one of their conditions. It took a while, since she wasn't the most organized little girl in the world. They finally called her into the living room, where they sat on the couch. Steffy sat on a chair, facing them. Her parents began telling their daughter what they expected of her and what she needed to do to earn a horse. Their baby girl asked whether she could grab a pencil and notebook to write everything down. Her parents smiled as they granted her permission. She quickly ran into her room and retrieved the objects. There was a lot to remember, and she couldn't afford to miss anything. Here are the rules her parents decided on:

Rule #1: Each of the three dogs should be walked on a daily basis.

Rule #2: Dog messes in the yard are to be cleaned up weekly.

Rule #3: The litter box and rodent cages needed to be cleaned weekly.

Rule #4: All pets needed to have fresh food and water daily.

Until now, Steffy had helped her parents with these chores but she had never been held solely responsible for doing them. Her parents were giving her a much bigger responsibility for the animals than she already had, in hopes that she would gain a better understanding of how much responsibility a horse would be. *Okay, I can handle this!* she thought. Then her dad added one more rule. It was huge. Steffy was very glad she was already sitting down when she heard it.

Rule #5: You will need to get straight A's on your report card.

It was as if a bomb had been dropped. Had Steffy really heard her dad correctly? Did he just say she needed to get a perfect report card to get a horse? The little second-grader sat there in shock. She desperately tried to think of something she could say to change their minds. She knew better than that, though, for the look on her dad's face made it perfectly clear that straight A's were a must. The only thing Steffy could do was take her dad's words, try to absorb them, and envision them in her head. Finally, after a few moments, she could see it. There she would be happy and smiling, her pets surrounding her as she stood there, looking at her parents. Her dad would be there, holding onto her horse, waiting for her to get it from him. Her mom would be standing next to him, smiling. Yes, she could see it all in her mind's eye. All of it, except that report card full of A's.

Steffy's dad could see the look of disbelief on his little girl's face. He finished what he was saying with his famous last words of encouragement. He told her what he had always told his girls when they needed hope. Tim said, "Wish upon a star! When you wish upon a star, your dreams come true!" In a very real way, that statement did give her some hope. That night Steffy took her dad's advice and went out into their backyard. She looked up into the vast, dark night sky and picked out the biggest, brightest star she could find. She closed her eyes tightly and wished with all her might, saying, "I wish I may … I wish I might…have this wish I wish tonight…I wish for the straight A's that it will take for me to earn a horse of my very own." And then Steffy said this prayer: "Dear Jesus, thank You for all of my pets. I love them so, so, so much! Please help me to study hard. Dad says that I need to get straight A's in school to get a horse. Thank You. Amen."

That summer Steffy worked very hard to complete every task and to follow every rule her parents had made. When her friends wanted to play, they quickly learned that her chores came first. They had two choices: either wait for their friend to finish her tasks or help her finish them. Most of them didn't have pets of their own, so they enjoyed helping her. This summer was full of lessons for Steffy to learn, and she learned them well. She became a much more responsible pet owner, and this quality was very important if she were to become a horse owner. Horses require a lot of care, attention, and maintenance. She was developing good habits that would stay with her for the rest of her life, and she would be a much better horse owner because of them.

★ CHAPTER 2 ★

Another Horseless Summer... *and Another... and Another...*

THIRD GRADE SEEMED to come sooner than she expected. And Steffy had to admit that her teacher scared her in a way. Her third-grade teacher was close to her own height, but despite being short, she meant business. She made it very clear to her class that third grade was going to be quite a transition from second grade. She stressed that they had all better take this year as seriously as she was going to. It was her way or "Get held back!" Those were the only two choices she had to offer. There were no two ways about it. Steffy had to buckle down and get serious. Her dream depended on it, and the intimidation of her teacher was almost more than she could stand.

One day she read the spelling words on the homework board. Her jaw dropped as she read the letters, V-O-L-C-A-N-O. She tried sounding the word out. "Vol-ca-no." Then she read, "Volcano!" Steffy was happy she was able to read this word. However, she realized third-grade words were a little more difficult than second-grade words. On another day, her teacher told the class to turn to page twenty-five in their math books. *No way,* Steffy thought as she read, *fractions and division...what could be more confusing than this?* By the end of the day, though, she was able to convince herself that she would be able to make it through the third grade. But her teacher wasn't exaggerating; third grade was going to be pretty tough.

Not only was the third-grader frustrated in the classroom, but she found herself equally as frustrated on the playground at recess time as well. One day she discovered some boys were torturing a helpless little

10

"Daddy Longlegger." Other children surrounded the boys, and they were all laughing. Steffy watched in horror as they harmed the little critter. Now would probably be a good time to mention that this little tomboy and her two sisters had been studying martial arts since she was five years old. This was well before the first *Karate Kid* movie came out on the big screen, mind you. To be honest, they were doing karate before karate was cool. Their dad was very protective of his girls, and he wanted to make sure they knew how to defend themselves. He was concerned about "stranger danger," so he found the best instructor in the county, and his daughters took private lessons from him three days a week. They learned eight different martial arts but focused mainly on karate, jujutsu and judo.

The three of them were firmly instructed never to use their skills on anyone, unless their lives depended on it. Steffy struggled with this thought for a moment, but she was determined to rescue the defenseless creature. She decided that judo was more of a form of wrestling than fighting. So she chose the biggest boy committing the cruel act, and she told him he had better stop what he was doing, or she would make him stop. The boy laughed at her. Without hesitation she grabbed him by his shirt and flipped him over her shoulder, throwing him flat on the ground. She had him in a neck hold and kept him there until he and all the other boys promised never to lay another finger on any helpless bugs ever again. Needless to say, she never saw another kid torture another bug. Not for the rest of that year or for any year after that.

Steffy's ninth birthday came and went. This year she didn't dream of getting a horse for her birthday, though. She knew she now had to earn one. Her report card had a couple of C's on it already, so she wasn't expecting much. Before she knew it, third grade was over, and summer was here. Even though she hadn't gotten a perfect report card, eliminating her chances of getting her horse, she still enjoyed her summer a lot. She bonded with her pets on a deeper level now that she had been caring for them solely by herself. She especially bonded with her cat. He was a gray and black tiger-striped tabby with a black mask painted on his face, hence his name, Bandit. He always seemed to need extra love and affection. Steffy's dad had found him as a kitten at the feed store just down the road from their home when she was five years old. From the moment the two met, they had been inseparable.

Steffy rocked her kitten every night in the rocking chair until he fell asleep. Those two just loved each other. In fact, it wasn't uncommon to see this little animal walk Steffy to school and wait for her outside her classroom window until school was over. Then his owner carried him all the way home. This little kitten grew to be quite a large cat. He never passed up a chance to eat. And if anyone accidentally left a box of doughnuts out on the table at night, you can bet your bottom dollar he finished off every single one by morning.

As summer neared its end, Steffy was confident that nothing was going to stop her from achieving a perfect report card. Once school started, that headstrong fourth-grader hit the books hard, at least until she and her classmates were introduced to their new gym teacher. As far as Steffy was concerned, that was the day when time stood still. His name was Mr. Minger, and the puppy-love-struck student was sure he was an exact replica of one of her lifelong heroes, Superman. He was tall and muscular, and he was as handsome as the Man of Steel himself. She was thoroughly convinced Mr. Minger was as close to Superman as she was ever going to get. Unfortunately, this crush worked as a major distraction for her and really affected her grades. But it was there, and that was that. There was no fighting it.

Wednesdays were gym class for Steffy. And as quickly as Clark Kent turned into Superman, this crush-driven fourth-grader changed from a tough tomboy, who practiced martial arts three nights a week, to a prissy young lady with long ringlet curls. Wednesdays were quickly referred to as "Minger Day" in the Hacker household. Everyone in the house knew when Minger Day was near, due to all the signs. For instance, the pink sponge rollers that could normally be found wrapped tightly in Sandy's hair somehow vanished after Steffy's bath; magically, becoming entwined in the fourth-grader's waist-long, bright-red hair.

Another sign to show the world that the next day was Minger Day was Steffy's sudden ability to lay out all her clothes the night before. And it was always the same outfit: her favorite powder-blue dress, her gym shorts, her white Sunday shoes, and her gym shoes. Steffy had it down to an art. While in class, she asked to go to the bathroom; then she changed into her gym clothes moments before she and her classmates walked to the school's gymnasium. Finally, one of the last signs to show the world, or at least her family, that Minger Day had arrived was the unmistakable look of puppy love in the young girl's sparkling blue eyes. In addition, she could be found falling asleep the night before with a great, big smile on her love-stricken face.

As you may have guessed, Steffy didn't achieve her goal of becoming a horse owner in fourth grade either. She learned the hard way that by losing focus of her goal, she lost the ability of achieving that goal. She spent another summer without a horse, wishing she had put more energy into her grades. This became especially true after she went with Darnelle and her family to the county fair. There were kids her age at the fair showing their horses. *That could be me out there in that showring! Why didn't I concentrate more on my grades?* she thought. Then she realized what she had to do, so she decided at that moment that she was going to get her mind off of Mr. Minger and back on her books.

Fifth grade was finally here, and the crush she had on her gym teacher eventually diminished. Steffy enveloped herself with every horse- and pony-related book in the entire school library. And once she exhausted all the equine resources there, she went on to do the same at the town's public library. One could almost always find her in one of the two places, reading about horse care, horse maintenance, and horse health. She also read about horse training, horse breeding, horse rescues, and horse showmanship. The fifth-grader learned all about how easily these animals could contract an illness. She learned first aid for horses and even started keeping a notebook of all she had learned through her reading. Practically every single book report she wrote that year had something to do with either horses or ponies.

Weather permitting, and depending on Darnelle's parents' schedule, they took the two horse-crazed girls to their niece's ranch as often as they could. The girls took turns grooming and riding Darnelle's cousin's horse. This mare was a spunky golden palomino, and Steffy learned a lot from that horse, like how to stay on, for instance. She loved those weekends out in the country with that animal. It was good for her to get more experience with horses, and it helped her to stay sane throughout her wait for a horse of her own. She and Darnelle fought like sisters over many ideas, but their love of animals, horses particularly, bonded them throughout their entire childhood.

By the end of the school year, Steffy's grades had improved tremendously. She had mostly A's and a few B's. She really had come a long way, and the knowledge of horses she had obtained was priceless. Although she was disappointed about not getting a horse of her own, she was proud of herself for getting her grades up and keeping her focus on her goal.

Something else happened this year that would change Steffy's life forever. While she was at church one Sunday, there was an altar call. Steffy had always gone to church, but she had never asked Jesus into her heart. On this particular Sunday, a woman walked up to her and asked her whether or not she was saved. Steffy told her she hadn't yet made that decision. The woman said to her, "I see you here at church whenever the doors are open, but you have never taken the opportunity to ask Jesus to be your Lord and Savior?"

Steffy answered, "I guess I just wasn't ever ready."

The woman went on to explain that if people don't ask Jesus to forgive their sins and ask Jesus to live in their heart, they won't go to heaven when they die. She and Steffy talked about heaven and death for a little while.

Steffy decided to go up front to the altar and accept God's gift of salvation. The woman said a "Sinner's Prayer." Steffy repeated it and meant it with all her heart. Then the woman smiled with a tear in her eye and gave Steffy a big hug. After that she said, "Welcome! You are now part of the family of God, and we are sisters in Christ."

Steffy was so happy. She ran back to the pew where Sandy was sitting. The brand-new Christian told her sister what had just transpired. Sandy was elated and hugged her little sister. When they got home, Steffy told the rest of her family all about it. They were so happy for her. Then she called all her friends and told them all about how she had gotten saved.

(There is a copy of this prayer in the back of this book. If you haven't yet taken this step, you can say this prayer in your own words. You must say it and mean it with your whole heart. You must promise to follow

Jesus the very best you can. If you do these things, you too will receive your ticket to heaven, and you will live with Jesus forever.)

It seemed as though God was always at work in this young girl's life, keeping her in close contact with horses. She was always grateful when He did this, and she always thanked Him for those "horsey opportunities." For instance, whenever Steffy's dad went to Michigan to visit his fellow pigeon club member, Rip, she tagged along to play with Rip's daughter, Lori. The two girls were the same age, and it just so happened that Lori had friends who owned horses. So while their dads hung out together, admiring pigeons, the girls took off in Lori's golf cart to find her horsey friends and go horseback riding. Every chance Steffy was given, she rode, and she became pretty good at it.

Her parents bought her a subscription to a horse magazine, and that girl soaked up horse knowledge like a sponge. They were starting to see their daughter was nowhere close to outgrowing her I-want-a-pony phase. Steffy finished the summer off by going to the county fair with Darnelle, just like she had done the previous summer. She walked through each of the three horse barns, carefully reading the name plates of each horse and rider. She looked at their pictures and saw how beautifully each stall was so carefully decorated. How she longed to be part of this world. She imagined herself on the back of her own horse in one of those photos. She could see herself sitting on a muscular barrel-racing champion, as fit and strong as the horses she had read about in the library books she had read. Maybe she would earn a golden palomino like Darnelle's cousin's horse or a black Arabian like the Black Stallion. She could only dream.

Steffy was now entering the sixth grade. The young cowgirl-wanna-be was growing a little disheartened. She began to wonder whether she would ever be able to get those grades and earn herself a horse. One Saturday afternoon her dad came home with a surprise for her. He drove up into the family's driveway in his old green van. He and his friend Rip had just gone to another flea market. He had bought some things for his little girl. She watched as he pulled three gifts out of the van. The first gift was a gently used red-and-black guitar.

"Every cowgirl needs one of these to play around a campfire as her horse drifts off to sleep," he said with a smile. Then he handed her the instrument. Steffy took the guitar and jumped up, giving her dad a kiss on his cheek. Her lips felt a bit funny from the touch of his scruffy face.

Then he removed from his van an old leather bridle with a rusty bit on the end of it and said, "Every cowgirl needs a bridle to put on her horse to guide it as she rides."

Steffy felt warm tears of joy flow down her freckled cheeks as she took the bridle from her dad's rough hands.

After that, he reached into his van and pulled out an old, worn pony saddle. "And every cowgirl needs her own saddle," he added with a smile.

Steffy couldn't stop the tears from flowing. "My own saddle too?" she asked as she took it from his hands.

Her dad replied, "Yep, Steffer. Just think, one day all of your hard work will pay off, and you will be putting a bridle and saddle on a horse of your very own."

His daughter held the old saddle in her hands. It was dry and tough, but it had the sweet smell of horses all over it. Steffy had the biggest smile on her face. She couldn't wait to show her mom and sisters her new presents.

The gifts brought Steffy some hope. She continued to grow stronger as a horse person, and her grades were getting better too. However, even with all her hard work, studying, and striving to get the grades she needed, she didn't get straight A's in sixth grade either. So once again, the little animal lover found herself lacking a horse. Her spirits were lifted when her grandma Mama Jo took her to a very dear Italian family, who were lifelong friends of hers. It just so happened that they also owned a beautiful golden palomino mare. Steffy had the privilege of riding this sweet animal that particular summer, and what an experience it was! She was used to a palomino that was high spirited and headstrong. But this mare was altogether different. When this precious horse saw a person with a saddle in her or his arms, she came galloping up, begging to be ridden. So Steffy did just that. Mama Jo took her to ride every other Sunday that summer. She also bought Steffy a membership at the local zoo to help keep her mind off her lack of a horse.

This devout animal lover arrived at the zoo every Monday through Friday that summer when the doors opened. Someone in her family dropped her off, and five to six hours later, someone else in her family picked her up. She couldn't get enough of those animals. Steffy made friends with the zookeepers, and she was given special permission to groom and clean up after the animals in the petting zoo area. She loved to brush and care for the horses, donkeys, goats, sheep, and others. Next to the equines, her favorite animals were the llamas. One llama in particular quickly became Steffy's all-time favorite. Every day when she arrived at the barnyard, she stretched out her arms and called to her. Instantly, the animal came galloping across the barnyard, right into Steffy's arms. The llama would get up close to the loving twelve-year-old, stretch out her long neck, and lay it across the girl's shoulder, pulling her in toward her and giving her a gentle, loving hug.

Every day that summer seemed to be filled with something new and exciting to learn at the zoo. All the animals had their own personalities. Each was unique in its own way. One day the female donkey gave birth to a colt. Steffy was in awe. The baby donkey was so precious. He was gray, and his tiny hooves were just a little bigger than the size of a quarter. This young animal lover had experienced a miracle, and she cherished that memory very much. She learned that a very big part of caring for a horse or pony or even a miniature donkey was cleaning up a lot of manure. That was the reality of it. Riding a horse was the fun part. But caring for the horse was a necessity and quite a big job, as she found out. That summer was unforgettable. All the knowledge she gained from the zoo would also help her in her horse ownership. The experience was invaluable. Every single bit of it was part of a master plan. However, like the summers before, it ended all too soon.

This new school year would be a lot different for Steffy. She was leaving the comfort zone of her elementary school, and she was being thrown smack-dab into a great big middle school. Everything she had known as a child was about to change. With this change came a whole new determination. By the time she received her last report card and completed seventh grade, Steffy's goal was to never again have to say, "I had another horseless summer … and another … and another …"

★ CHAPTER 3 ★

ᘓ⊙ᕽ   *Steffy's Prayer*   ᕽ⊙ᘔ

S EVENTH GRADE WAS staring Steffy straight in the face. She held her sixth-grade report card in her hands as she waited for the city bus to arrive at the bus stop. It was her first day of middle school, and she was a little nervous, to say the least. She held onto that report card to remind herself that this was a whole new year. She promised herself right then and there that she was going to achieve her goal *this* year. "Look out, seventh grade!" Steffy said to herself. "I'm getting straight A's this year if I have to study my guts out, have no life at all, and become a permanent fixture on the library wall. I am getting a horse this year, and *nothing's* going to stop me!" She was as serious as she had ever been.

It was the mid-1980s now, and big hair and parachute pants were the style. The boys hung out with the boys, and the girls hung out with the girls here in junior high school. This made Steffy a little more than irritated. She was a tomboy, and she had been a player in flag football with the boys in elementary school rather than a cheerleader on the sidelines with the girls. Things were different now. During homeroom she still arm-wrestled with the boys, and she usually won. But other than that, it just wasn't cool to be seen hanging out with the guys anymore. The middle schooler missed flag football and sticking up for "Daddy Longleggers." Becoming a young lady was harder than she had imagined.

She was convinced that middle school was completely overrated. Girls were full of drama the seventh-grader tried to avoid. But somehow it managed to find her. She had to defend herself against lies, and she had to keep the bullies at a distance. Life just wasn't as fun as it had been in elementary school. God is amazing, though, and He supplies our every need. Just in the nick of time, Steffy met a friend she would have for the rest of her life. She was a thin, blonde-haired, green-eyed girl named Cheryl. They met through Darnelle and became instant best friends. They stuck by each other, easing a lot of tension for them both as they adjusted to their lives as seventh-graders.

Cheryl learned of Steffy's determination to get straight A's on her report card. She encouraged her to study and do really well in school. She supported her one hundred percent. You could find the two of them either passing out newspapers on Cheryl's paper route in Cheryl's neighborhood or walking Steffy's dogs in Steffy's neighborhood. They lived across the river from each other, but the distance didn't stop them. Whatever they were doing, they were usually doing it together. The two best friends joined the track and field team together, and both of them did really well. But one thing never changed, and that was Steffy's determination to get that horse she'd always dreamed of. Cheryl helped her in any way she could, from quizzing Steffy before her tests to turning off the radio so Steffy could study when they stayed the night at each other's houses. Cheryl was a true friend through and through.

Before Steffy knew it, seventh grade was nearing its end, and she felt like she needed straight A's on her report card more than she needed air. She felt confident she would get a really good progress report this time, but a good one wasn't enough. She needed perfect grades. Nothing less would do. Her birthday snuck up on her, and suddenly she was a teenager. Her parents threw her a huge private party at a pizza parlor. She had over a dozen friends in attendance, and all of them had a blast. She had a cake decorated with horses, and this happy birthday girl thought her special day was all kinds of perfect.

Unfortunately, it seemed to fly by, along with Christmas and New Year's. With each grading period, the unfortunate girl just missed her goal with all A's and two B's. She couldn't seem to get those B's any higher. They were in Math and Biology, her two most difficult classes. Suddenly, the last day of seventh grade was here, and Steffy had to take her report card to every class and have each teacher put her grade on it. It would take almost all school day before she would find out what all her grades were. The suspense of it was almost more than she could stand, but the red-haired teenager had no choice. This was how the school did things, and she soon realized she would just have to deal with it.

With her report card in hand, Steffy went into each classroom holding her breath. She was unable to think of anything else except what grade each teacher was going to put on that card. English, Physical Education, Home Economics, Social Studies, Choir—every class she went into was sheer suspense. And in all of these classes, she received an A. Finally, she went into her Math class, and to her surprise she had raised her B to an A. She was so happy! But there was one more class she had to go to, one more grade she needed to get, and that was in Biology.

This was Steffy's favorite class. She wanted to become a veterinarian someday, and science intrigued her. She simply loved it. However, this subject didn't come easily to her, and at times she struggled to maintain a good grade. She was definitely concerned she may not get an A. If she was right, she wasn't going to be able to shake off the disappointment like she had so many years before. Steffy had worked harder this year than ever before to get a horse. If she didn't get one this summer, she was sure she would just explode.

So here she was, walking into her Biology classroom as tense as she could be. She bit her lower lip and prayed the whole time that somehow, some way, she would get an A in this one last class. She walked up to her teacher's desk and could almost hear a drumroll as she handed her report card to the educator. Her teacher wrote down a grade and handed it back to her. Steffy walked back to her seat, and then she took a deep breath before looking at it.

When she saw her grade, she fell into her seat. There she sat, more upset than she had ever been about grades in her entire life. Steffy stared at a B+. She felt her face getting red hot as she kept telling herself she should have worked harder. The very emotional girl couldn't stop the tears from pouring out of her eyes, and she let her face fall into her hands. She sobbed for what seemed like a very long time.

Finally, she felt her teacher's hand on her shoulder. "Honey, I gave you all the credit that I could, but I was only able to give you a B+. I am so sorry," her teacher said in a soft voice. When Steffy was finally able to catch her breath, she looked up at the woman. The other students had all left to go home—all except Cheryl, that is, who waited in the classroom doorway for her best friend.

"Now I will *never* get a horse! I have been trying since the second grade. I can't try any harder. I can't go through this again!" Steffy said to her teacher. Then Cheryl came into the classroom and gave her best friend a hug. She asked Steffy if she wanted to walk with her part way home, since all the city buses had already left the school grounds. Steffy nodded. Cheryl had a look of pity on her face. She knew how hard her best friend had strived for a perfect report card.

Just then Steffy's Biology teacher asked Steffy to wait a minute. The teacher went back to her desk and wrote something down on a piece of paper. She folded the paper and asked Steffy to give it to her parents when she got home. Fighting back her tears, the sad teenager put the note in her report card without looking at it. Then her teacher gave her a hug before she left.

Well, that's that then. No horse again this year. Just another year with an imperfect report card, she thought. She had never come that close before … all A's and one B+. The sad, horseless cowgirl began her long walk with her best friend. They walked down Main Street and past the cemetery. The sad teenager wondered how many of those people had accomplished their goals before they took their last breath. Then she began to wonder whether she would ever accomplish hers. And if she did, how much longer would it take? It had already been five whole years. She hated the thought of having to wait any longer.

When the traffic cleared, the two girls walked across Jefferson Boulevard, and then they walked over the railroad tracks. The next street was the one Cheryl lived on, so the girls gave each other a hug goodbye. Cheryl started on her way home, and then she turned around. "I will see ya later. Maybe we can do something tomorrow," she said, trying to sound positive.

Steffy forced a smile. "Okay," she answered. As she turned to head home, the disheartened teenager saw a building next to the railroad tracks. It was a feed store. "I bet they have grain in there. I bet they sell hay," the sad girl said to herself. Then she continued walking past the store, getting a little choked up again.

A few blocks farther down the street, she passed the church where her oldest sister, Sandy, had asked Jesus into her heart at the age of seven. This was the church they had attended regularly ever since Steffy was three years old. As the sad thirteen-year-old walked past the church, she wondered whether it would be completely selfish of her to vent to God about her situation. She decided to speak to Him.

"Lord, I know that there are kids in this world who are starving. I feel selfish right now for even asking, but am I *ever* gonna get a horse?" Steffy asked. She longed so badly for a horse of her own. "God," she continued, "I know I don't need a horse to survive. But sometimes I *feel* like I do, as selfish as it sounds to hear myself say it. But You know my heart. You created me with this love for horses." The tears started to well up in her eyes again.

But just then she remembered a Bible story in the Old Testament. It was about a woman who had desired to have something very precious. She'd wanted it so desperately that she prayed and prayed until she lost her voice. Someone even accused her of being drunk because she could no longer speak. But she kept on praying anyway. Her name was Hannah, and she asked the Lord for a baby. What Hannah wanted more than anything else in the entire world was a child of her very own. To be a mommy was her heart's desire. So she told God that if she could have a baby, she would give her baby back to Him. Sure enough, God honored her prayer, and she finally had a son! She raised her son up to love God and when he came of age, she sent him to live in the temple and serve God. (This story is found in the Bible, in the Old Testament book of 1 Samuel, the whole first chapter.)

I wonder, Steffy thought. Then she prayed with a smile on her face and a renewed hope in her heart. "Lord, just like Hannah, when I *do* get a horse, I want to give it back to you. I'm not sure how, but I will. I promise!" She was so excited about this new promise that she had made to God that she almost forgot she was sad. She kept on walking. Only now her tears were drying up, and she had a great big smile on her face. She would keep praying, but she wasn't as sad now. She had this joy inside her spirit. She was determined that when she did get her horse, she was going to give her gift back to God.

Steffy prayed the rest of the way home, asking God for her heart's desire. She knew her grades weren't good enough, but she continued to pray like Hannah had prayed anyway. When she finally got home, even though she was sad, she had peace inside that kept her from falling apart. She didn't know why she wasn't bawling her eyes out anymore. She knew only that her new promise to God had made her very happy. She would always remember it as "Steffy's Prayer."

Once she got to her house, her dogs were very excited to see her. Each was wagging its tail and licking her face at the same time. Steffy completed her chores and waited for her parents to come home from work. She was lying in the lush, soft grass in the backyard, with a dog on either side of her. The smallest one was in her arms. Her cat purred happily close by, rubbing his head up against her legs.

The thirteen-year-old lay on her back, looking up into the clear, blue sky. She was barefoot now, and she could feel the cool grass between her toes. She felt a tear run down the side of her face as she thought about not getting a horse again this year. The tear was followed by a smile, though, because she knew that when she did get that horse, she was going to keep her promise to God and give it back to Him. The thought of it was just so completely amazing that it made for a very bittersweet moment.

Her parents arrived home from work at the same time. They couldn't help but smile as they noticed their daughter lying on the ground, with all her pets loving on her. Steffy sat up slowly, setting her small dog down in the grass. As she stood up, her parents had already made their way into the yard. She pulled the report card out of her back pocket. Then she handed it to them, and the tears began welling up in her big blue eyes. Her parents knew what those tears meant, and their hearts broke for her. They were very quiet as they looked at the report card. They saw it had all A's and one B+. Their hearts sank, and they both got choked up too.

Then Steffy's dad noticed a folded-up piece of paper. "What is this?" he asked as he took out the note from Steffy's Biology teacher.

"I don't know," Steffy answered. "It's something my teacher wrote. She wanted me to give it to you guys."

Her dad read the note from beginning to end, and then he handed it to her mom. A big smile came across his face, and he looked at his wife and nodded. Sharon smiled too and nodded back at her husband.

Then they both looked at their baby. "Well, that settles it. Let's go horse shopping," her dad said with delight.

His confused little girl could hardly see his face through her tear-filled eyes. She swallowed really hard, looking as sad as could be. "But I didn't get all A's. I can't get a horse," she replied.

Her dad smiled. "Yes, you did!" He handed the note back to her, and this is what she read:

Dear Mr. & Mrs. Hacker, I couldn't let this last day of school go by without telling you something very important. Your daughter worked her very hardest to obtain an A in my class. My Biology class is not easy, and as far as I am concerned, this B+ is an A in my eyes. I just thought you might want to know that. Thank you, Mrs. B.

"Well, what can I say? If this B+ is an A in your teacher's eyes, then it's an A in my eyes too," he told her. "You worked so hard these past five years and this last year especially. You have proven to me that you have what it takes to make a great horse owner. I have complete faith in you. I am really proud of you, Steffer. You did it!"

Steffy just stood there. She couldn't speak. She couldn't get a word to form and fall from her lips. She almost lost her balance, standing there, so she took a couple of steps to the right and then caught herself. Her dad and mom chuckled to themselves, and then she began crying tears of happiness. Her parents wrapped their arms around her, they were getting a little emotional too.

Their daughter looked up at them. "I'm getting a horse! I am finally getting a horse of my very own!" Steffy shouted again and again.

The feelings of happiness and joy she experienced at that moment were almost overwhelming. This was one of the most incredible moments she had ever experienced up to this point in her life—next to getting saved, that is. Then she smiled as she thought, *This is even better than Minger Day!*

★ CHAPTER 4 ★

 Horses 101

HE FIRST PERSON Steffy called was her cousin Jason out in Pennsylvania. When he heard the news she was finally getting a horse, he screamed with excitement and jumped up and down. He couldn't wait to tell his parents. His dad was beside himself. In fact, he had to talk to Steffy's dad on the phone to verify the news. Both men, Steffy's dad and Jason's dad, were two of the biggest penny pinchers in the family. So when Steffy's dad had promised to get her a horse all those years ago, Jason's dad had reacted in disbelief. After all, horses are quite expensive. So back when Steffy was in the second grade, he vowed, "If Hacker gets Steffy a horse, that will be the day that I get Jason one." Now that day was here, and he had to make good on his word. So he and Jason were going horse shopping too.

That thirteen-year-old girl could have been mistaken for a news reporter. She called all the people she could think of. The excited teenager told everyone, from her sisters to her mom's entire side of the family in Pennsylvania. Then she called her dad's side of the family in Tennessee. She told everyone she had come in contact with, including the cashier at the grocery store and even the attendant at the gas station later that day. Finally, she called her closest friends, Cheryl and Darnelle.

Cheryl was ecstatic. She had been thinking this whole time that Steffy was going to spend another summer without a horse. She thought of all the time she had spent trying to help her best friend study. She remembered how high Steffy's hopes had been, and she recalled how crushed they both had been when they left the school that day. Now Cheryl was laughing and screaming with excitement over the phone.

She couldn't believe it. She was crying tears of happiness when she heard the wonderful news.

Darnelle was happy for Steffy too, although the news was a little bittersweet for her. She was now the horseless cowgirl. She had grown up with horses her whole life, and now that she and her parents were living in town, she didn't have a horse of her own. She had her cousin's horses to ride. But as grateful as she was for that, it still wasn't the same. Steffy could hear a hint of sadness in her friend's voice, maybe even some jealousy. But all in all, Darnelle was happy for her. She also had known of Steffy's hard work. She knew her friend had worked very hard to earn a horse. Darnelle also felt that if anyone deserved this moment of happiness, it was that redhead on the other end of the phone.

Steffy and her parents decided they would have to come up with a creative plan as to where they were going to keep this new member of the family. None of them had any idea where in the world they were going to put a horse, so they sat in the living room and brainstormed for a little while. They finally came up with some very good ideas. Maybe they could lease some property and put a small barn on it. That sounded like a pretty good idea. Or maybe they would have to find a barn that boarded horses. They weren't sure yet, but they did know one thing: they needed to find a place to keep a horse before they went out and actually purchased one.

Then out of the blue, Steffy's cousin Jason and his family made a surprise visit from Pennsylvania. Jason's and Steffy's older siblings hung out together, doing older teenage activities, while the two youngest horse-crazed cousins spent all their time dreaming about what types of horses they were going to buy. Both of their moms were busy making plans for meals and trips to the mall. Meanwhile, their dads were still scratching their heads. They were trying to grasp the realization that they were at the beginning stages of investing in some very pricey pets for their babies.

A week of having family fun and catching up had gone by rather quickly, and Jason's family finally had to go back home. Jason invited Steffy to come out to Pennsylvania with them for the summer. However, Steffy couldn't imagine leaving her three dogs, cat, and rodents behind. Then Jason said, "My neighbors have two ponies, and we can ride them any time we want to!" Suddenly, Steffy found herself kissing her larger-sized pets goodbye as her parents assured her that her animals would be well taken care of while she was gone. They also assured her that the minute they found a place to keep a horse, Steffy would be back on the turnpike, headed home.

Her aunt proved her love for her niece by putting up with having Steffy's rodents in her vehicle during the entire 640 miles back to Pennsylvania. The deal was that her animal-loving niece would have to keep her pet mice and rat at another cousin's house for the summer. She would need to go there every few days to care for them. The excited teenager agreed without hesitation. She loved being in Pennsylvania with her mom's side of the family. Being out in the country and surrounded by loving family members, she knew this was where she wanted to be. She decided right then and there that this was going to be one memorable summer, and it was.

She stayed at Jason's house during the first two weeks, and the two cousins rode the neighbor's ponies every day. All day long, they rode through the countryside and into town. They pretended to be a cowgirl and a cowboy out on the range. They were up at the crack of dawn every day, grooming, feeding, riding, and enjoying their summer ponies together. It was their dream, and they were living it to the fullest. They also spent a large part of their days cleaning out a section of Jason's barn, getting it ready for his new horse. The two cousins were simply having the time of their lives.

Steffy's mom had five sisters and two brothers, and it seemed that each of their youngest created quite a bond with each other. Jason was the youngest in his family, with a burning love for horses. That and the fact that his Indiana cousin was a tomboy made them the best of friends. He also had to share her with their other cousins, so every two weeks Steffy took turns with each of the other three. Her pet rodents were at her older cousin, Larry's house, and as God planned it, he was married to a horse-crazed equestrian named Ami. It just so happened that Ami worked at a horse race track. She was a groom, and she cared for very expensive race horses, Thoroughbreds.

This thirteen-year-old was about to experience something only God Himself could have arranged. She liked to refer to it as "Horses

101." The time she spent with Ami was indispensable. The experience took her knowledge of horses to a whole new level. Ami took Steffy with her every day to work for two weeks at a time. They were up at four o'clock every morning. After breakfast, they rushed out the door with a cup of hot tea in their hands. Then they were literally "off to the races." Steffy's heart beat a little faster every time they entered the racing grounds. She could smell the mixture of horse sweat, oiled leather, and sweet feed as they drove in. When the horse-crazed teenager jumped out of Ami's car, she could feel the thunder of hooves hitting the ground under her feet as the horses exercised on the track. It was always still dark out by the time they reached the track. And as the sun came up, its light gave birth to an entire world of fascinating horses.

The barn where Ami worked housed dozens of Thoroughbreds, and Ami was assigned to a dozen of her own. Steffy found out just how much work horses really are. The lessons she learned that summer were priceless. These race horses were pampered and cared for to the extreme. Ami taught Steffy that this was how she was to care for her horse when she got one of her own. Ami taught her little cousin the importance of scrubbing out a horse's water bucket to remove harmful bacteria that can make a horse sick. In addition, she taught her how to make sure the water bucket was hung up properly so the horse couldn't knock it off the stall wall. "A horse must always have fresh, clean water to drink because horses without fresh water can colic. And colic in the horse world can be another name for death!" Ami said.

Ami continued teaching Steffy the basics of horse care. She explained that a good horse owner is serious about a clean stall. "Don't ever go one day without cleaning your horse's stall thoroughly." Ami told her. She gave Steffy a pitchfork and had her mimic everything she did. Her little cousin learned exactly how to properly do the job. "If you fail to clean your horse's stall this well, your horse could end up with serious hoof diseases. Make no mistake about it, horses have had to be put down or killed due to their owner's negligence." Next, this knowledgeable horsewoman taught this teenage horse lover how to properly groom a horse.

"Brushing a horse properly will keep his coat healthy and free of dirt that could get trapped under the saddle and cause saddle sores," she explained thoroughly.

Ami went on to say, "You must always remember to pick your horse's hooves before and after you ride him." She demonstrated on one of the Thoroughbreds by lifting each hoof. Using the hoof pick properly, she carefully pointed it away from the horse's leg as she picked each hoof. Then she handed Steffy the hoof pick and had her do the same. After that Ami taught Steffy some behavior skills. She said, "Make the horses mind you. Don't let them get away with anything. Horses are like little kids. They will try to be naughty just to see how much they can get away with. They can be killing machines as well. Make sure that you have full control of the horse and make him obey you." This woman was meticulous about how she cared for and handled horses. She wanted Steffy to adopt these high standards of care as well. She wanted to help her grow into the fine horsewoman she knew she could be.

Ami was a perfectionist. She strived to be the best wife, mother, daughter, friend, aunt, cousin, equestrian, and animal owner she could be. And at Steffy's tender age of thirteen, she wanted to instill these good habits into her as well. Ami showed her little cousin how to properly care for a horse, and she had Steffy bathing, grooming, feeding, watering, and cleaning up after four horses every day. It was like boot camp for a horse lover. Even though Steffy's hands were covered in blisters and her muscles ached, she thought it was great. She knew she was getting the best training possible. She was very grateful.

Ami also treated Steffy to English horseback riding lessons. She bought Steffy her first riding helmet, and she let her borrow her riding boots and clothes. Steffy had only ever ridden western and bareback. English was quite a bit different with the fancy posting and jumping. She loved it. She even got Jason out there for some riding lessons. It was quite the summer. That urban cowgirl felt at home in the barn. The work was hard, but she loved every minute of it. She knew she was where she was supposed to be. She wasn't a cowgirl-gonna-be; she was a cowgirl. From her dusty red hair to her blistered-up hands, right down to her muddy boots, she was all country. It was how God had created her to be, back when He'd formed her in her mother's body. It was all part of His master plan.

Steffy spent two weeks with each of her other three closest cousins, who happened to be the babies of their families too: Monika, Lori and Leslie. They also were young teenage girls, and their time together was spent curling hair, applying makeup, dressing up, reading each other's diaries (with permission, of course), and talking about boys. The last two weeks of summer were upon her, and Steffy elected to spend them with Jason. The two imagined what their lives might be like when they got older. "We are going to have Jason & Steffy's Stables!" the two dreamed.

One day, Jason invited Steffy to church camp. She happily tagged along and had a ton of fun up in the Ephrata Mountains with her cousin. They rode horses, had a race, and built campfires; and she met a lot of new people. They also watched a couple of movies that would change Steffy's life forever.

You see, back when Steffy was eleven years old, she'd asked Jesus into her heart. But when she did that, she had a limited understanding of her salvation. She got saved because she essentially wanted to avoid going to "H-E-Double Hockey Sticks" when she died. She didn't realize she was missing out on a very big blessing. At the end of the first day at camp, the kids were treated to the first movie. It was about a troubled boy who came very close to losing his life and how he found Jesus. Ultimately, he led his cousin to know Him too. The movie touched Steffy's heart so much, and it caused her eyes to be opened spiritually. She was finally beginning to understand that God loved her more than she ever knew. Jesus had come to earth to die for her sins so she could have a relationship with God, not fear Him and walk on eggshells for the rest of her life.

She finally began to see God as her heavenly Father and Best Friend, not just her Judge. She knew now He loved her more than anyone could ever possibly love her and that He wanted to have a relationship with her. She'd never looked at her salvation that way before. This was a whole new world for this teenage Christian. Steffy took a walk by herself and talked to God like He was the only one up there on that mountain with her. It was such a beautiful experience. She rededicated her life to God that night and had a wonderful time getting to really know Him. When she and Jason got home from camp, they had a lot to talk about. She shared her experience with her sister Sandy over the phone. Sandy read Bible scriptures to her little sister, reflecting God's love. Then she promised to help her grow closer to Jesus once Steffy got back to Indiana.

A couple of days later, Steffy got a phone call from her dad. "Steffer!" he said. "I have some great news! My friend Chuck knows of someone who will rent some land out to us for a horse. It's his daughter, and she has a dairy farm."

Before she knew it, Jason was helping her pack her things, and she and her Pennsylvania family were saying goodbye. Both cousins were so focused on their "horses to be" that saying goodbye this time wasn't too terribly difficult. Steffy's other cousins were super excited for them as well. And even though they knew it would be a while before they would see Steffy again, they knew soon she was going to become a horse owner. And they couldn't have been happier for her. It was near the end of the summer now, and Steffy was excited to get back to Indiana. She couldn't believe she was going to see the place where she would be keeping a horse. She was literally one step away from getting a horse of her own. After visiting this dairy farm and figuring out all the details of keeping a horse there, Steffy would finally get to start horse shopping. She was so excited that she could hardly stand it.

★ CHAPTER 5 ★

ᏮᎬ A Star at Last ᎬᏮ

A FEW DAYS AFTER being home, the animal-crazed teenager finally finished unpacking and getting reacquainted with her three dogs and cat. She put her rodents back in their places in her room. In addition, she made sure to take all three of her dogs on very long walks. After that, her cat got extra rocking chair time with her. Then she, her dad, and his friend Chuck drove up to visit Chuck's daughter, Missy, on her dairy farm. It was a beautiful summer day—not too hot, not too cool, but just right. It was a forty-five-minute drive down to Woodland, Indiana, and by the time they got there, Steffy's heart was racing with excitement.

As they reached the long driveway leading to the farmhouse, she could smell the "fresh country air," as her mom called it. It reminded her of Pennsylvania. She could hear the barking of dogs and the mooing of cows getting louder the closer they got. When they parked, the happy animal lover was in a hurry to meet Missy's dogs. Likewise, the dogs greeted her with kisses and tail wags, like they had known her their whole lives. Missy came out of the house with a smile. She introduced herself to Steffy and her dad. Then she gave her dad, Chuck, a great big hug.

"So," she said to Steffy, "you like horses, huh?" The young cowgirl smiled and nodded shyly. "Well, we have land here, and you are welcome to keep a horse out here if you promise to follow all the rules of the farm, okay?"

Steffy answered, "Yes, ma'am!"

Missy went on to tell her about the rules and describe what she expected of her. Then Steffy asked, "Do you have any horses on this farm right now?" After all, this was a farm, and there was bound to be a horse or two around there somewhere. The thirteen-year-old was chomping at the bit, so to speak, at the thought of getting near another horse. And as far as she was concerned, the sooner she could see another equine, the better.

"Well, we do have a very old pony over in the steer corral," Missy began. "Her owners had rescued her and brought her here in terrible shape, hoping to help her. Her hooves are overgrown, and she is too wild to let anyone trim them. We agreed to let her owners keep her here. But shortly after they got the poor mare here, they fell on some hard times and couldn't afford to care for her. The humane thing to do now is to put her out of her misery. She is obviously sick, so that's the plan."

"May I see her?" Steffy asked with concern.

"Sure," Missy answered, "but I doubt she will let you get very close."

As Missy led Steffy to the steer corral, the inquiring teenager was filled with curiosity. She was a little anxious to meet the orphaned animal. When they reached their destination, Steffy was unable to spot the pony at first.

"She's right over there," Missy said, pointing in one direction.

"I don't see her," the young girl replied, looking among the steers.

"She blends right in with them. She is a black-and-white pinto pony. Keep looking. You'll see her."

Nothing could have prepared Steffy for what she finally saw. She discovered a tiny pony's head attached to an incredibly overweight, matted body, covered in dried mud. All the color rushed from the girl's face. She slowly made her way to the tall metal gate, which separated her from the wretched little animal.

Without taking her eyes off the small mare, the teenager slowly grabbed the gate in front of her. She held onto it tightly. Her heart sank as she studied the pony. Missy was talking, but Steffy didn't hear one word. She thought *this animal is severely overweight. I'm sure that she has founder.* Steffy remembered well what this disease was. Founder is a hoof disease caused by overeating. It makes the hoof swell with infection. There is a small bone inside the hoof, called a coffin bone. If the founder is severe enough, the coffin bone rotates. If it rotates more than eleven degrees, the injury is irreversible, and the animal won't recover; sadly it must be humanely destroyed.

Steffy's eyes immediately went from the pony's fat belly to her hooves. The mud was deep because it had rained the night before. Because of this, Steffy didn't expect to get a good look at them. Then she noticed four hornlike structures poking up out of the mud in front of where the mare's hooves would be. They were so long that the tips of them were flush with the pony's knees. Steffy's jaw dropped, and her eyes widened as she asked, "Um … are those … her hooves?" She had a very worried look on her face.

"Yeah, those sure are," Missy answered sadly. "The blacksmiths weren't ever able to handle her well enough to get them trimmed. We had several of them out here. After getting bit and kicked enough times, they all just gave up."

The site of that animal took Steffy back in her memory to pictures she had seen in horse books—photographs of neglected horses and ponies and what could happen when hooves are left untrimmed. An equine should have its hooves trimmed every four to six weeks. This little mare must have gone without hoof care for years for them to look this bad. Realizing this, Steffy was almost sure the pony must have thrush as well. Thrush is a hoof disease caused by careless cleaning of the hoof. Mud, manure, and moisture get trapped in the hoof, causing bacteria to grow. This, over time, slowly rots the hoof.

The compassionate teenager's heart swelled with pity for the mangy pony. She tried hard to swallow a lump in her throat that just wouldn't go down. Then she put her left hand over her heart; she could almost feel it breaking. Suddenly, the Holy Spirit spoke to the young girl. Instantly she knew it wasn't by accident that she had stumbled on this needy pony; it was by divine appointment. It was all part of God's plan. At that moment she understood why God had sent her there. It wasn't for any other reason than to bring her and this pony together. This was no coincidence. This was a "God-incidence."

Without thinking twice, Steffy spoke up. "How much do you want for her?"

Missy looked shocked and somewhat confused. Then she answered her, saying, "Um … what?"

The serious teenager repeated, "How much do you want for her?"

Now Tim and Chuck had been standing nearby about the time

Steffy first spotted the pony. They too had seen the pinto and were talking about the sad-looking animal amongst themselves. They agreed that Missy should put that poor thing out of its misery soon. Steffy had never heard them, though. She'd been too busy studying the little mare.

Missy was a little unsure whether she wanted to burden this young girl with such a project. But then she saw the look of love and concern in Steffy's eyes. Finally, Missy heard herself say, "Well, you can have her if you want her. But I can't guarantee that you will be happy with this decision. This pony is in bad shape."

Tim just stood there, listening to their conversation. He was caught off guard when he heard his daughter ask Missy the question. In addition, he was concerned by what his little girl might be getting herself into. Then he heard his daughter say, "So she's *mine?*"

Missy nodded and said, "Yeah, if you want her."

Without hesitation, the ecstatic teenager began climbing the tall metal gate, skipping some bars as she went, to get to the top as fast as she could. When she reached the top, she threw herself over, dropping into the muddy corral with a splash.

The cattle quickly scattered, leaving the startled pony all alone to fend for herself. She tried to run from the newcomer, but she only tripped over her overgrown hooves. The pitiful mare's limp took Steffy's breath away, and her heart ached for her. Steffy gathered her thoughts and decided she must be very patient and soft spoken to gain this pony's trust. The young equestrian was so excited to finally meet the pony she had worked five years to earn. This was the moment she had been waiting for all these years, and it was way better than she had ever imagined.

Steffy squatted down as far to the ground as she could without sitting in the mud. She wanted to appear less threatening to the old girl. The two watched each other motionlessly. At last, the pony seemed a little more curious. Now that Steffy was still, the pony may have felt as though she had more control over the situation. She seemed less fearful.

Everything Steffy had ever read regarding the trust between a horse or pony and its owner was brought back to her memory. For every moment Steffy sat there, looking into her pony's eyes, she remembered one skill after another about how to communicate with her. All this information was crucial to their relationship. The next few moments and the next few days would play a critical role in how the two developed as a team.. Steffy knew this, and she let her pony take as much time as she needed.

Curiosity seemed to have gotten the better of the animal, and the wide-eyed little mare decided to investigate this interesting human. Slowly she inched her way toward Steffy. At last, she was within arm's length of her. The shy, timid pinto stretched out her thick neck and drew in a big breath of air. That way she could get a good whiff of this compelling new stranger. The pony was so adorable as she stood there, watching Steffy ever so closely. Her little head bobbed up and down as she took in Steffy's scent. To Steffy's surprise, the pony stretched out her lips to nuzzle the teenager's hand. Steffy was thrilled. This was her pony's signal that she was accepting her. The little mare sensed the girl's excitement, and she let out a long whinny. It was so high pitched and precious that it made Steffy smile.

As the pony called out, her little head shook, causing the hair on her forehead to move from side to side. Then something caught Steffy's eye. *What's that?* she thought. She saw something white on the pony's face, under her forelock or bangs. She reached up very slowly toward her pony's forehead. The little animal was still very nervous, but something about Steffy's caring nature caused her to trust. The curious girl carefully brushed the animal's forelock to the side of her fuzzy black face. She immediately grinned when she discovered a white spot in the middle of her pony's forehead. This marking is called a "star."

Missy saw what Steffy was looking at, and with a smile, she called out to the teenager, "They called her Star!"

Smiling back, Steffy said to herself, "My pony's name is Star." Then she felt goose bumps form up and down her arms. She looked at her pony and said, "All these years I have been wishing on a star ... and now, here you are!"

She held her little mare's precious face in her hands. "Star," she said softly, "you are *my* pony now. I am going to love you until you love me back. Then after that, I am going to love you for the rest of your life."

She slowly stood up, and without lifting her hands off her pony, she cautiously patted Star's neck. Then she softly patted her shoulders and then her front legs. After that she ran her hands along Star's potbelly, down each back leg, and up over her rump. When she finished, she began the process backward. She patted Star along her other side, up over her rump, down each hind leg, under her little, fat belly, down each front leg, and up her neck until she was holding Star's face in her hands again. She was imprinting on her. She was bonding with her.

Steffy looked into Star's big brown eyes, outlined in blue, and promised her, "Star ... you are *my* pony now, and you are going to get better, and we are going to be best friends. I have waited so long for you. I have prayed so hard for you." Then she gave her pony a gentle hug.

Missy was amazed that Star stood there while her new owner handled her like she did. She began to have hope for that little mare after all. Missy smiled as she watched the two together, and she called out, "I have some treats for your pony!" Then she motioned for Steffy to follow her.

Tim just watched. He was completely confused about the whole pony transaction, and he couldn't yet find the words to say to his daughter about the entire ordeal. So he waited, he watched, and he listened. Then he talked to Chuck about it. Meanwhile, Steffy saw Missy disappear into the house. She heard footsteps fade in the distance. Missy had gone down to her basement, and shuffling and banging could be heard. The teenager waited outside since her boots and the bottom edges of her pants were covered in mud.

"I'll be right up!" she hollered. "I have a couple of things here that the last owner left behind." As Missy emerged from the dark cellar, she carried an old wooden brush box covered in dust. "It isn't much," she said with a smile, "but it'll get you started."

Steffy returned the smile as Missy handed her the box. The curious cowgirl found one old brush, one very used comb, one rusty hoof pick, and a small, rusty O-ring pony bit. The young teenager smiled as she took the old wooden box and all its contents from the sweet woman. She was extremely grateful. Steffy stopped and looked up into the bright July sky to thank God for the little mare she now owned. The sky was baby blue, and it was also crystal clear, except for one small cloud. It was a peculiar-looking little cloud, all wispy and sort of swirly. It wasn't billowy or soft looking like a typical cloud. It was more like a mist.

"Hmmm ... a mist ... that's pretty ... star mist," Steffy said to herself. "I know! How about Starlight Mist? And just like my name, I will spell her name differently too; it will be spelled Starlite Mist."

Then she prayed, "Thank You, God! She's *perfect!*" The warm sun kissed Steffy's round face softly, as if God were saying, *You're welcome.* She noticed her dad was standing there, looking completely puzzled. He watched his daughter walk up to him, and he just stared at her. Then his eyes shifted to the half-dead pony standing in the corral. He studied her for a moment. Then he looked back at his little girl.

Finally, he said in a soft voice, "Steffer? Um, I remember telling you that you could have any horse you wanted." Then he cleared his throat. "I thought you had your heart set on a champion barrel racer or a prize-winning pole bender. Why in the world would you want to exchange an amazing horse like that for a pony like this?"

Steffy looked down at her muddy boots and drew in a big breath. She gently kicked a small pebble with her right boot and let out a long sigh. Finally, she tightened her grip around the handle of the brush box with one hand and adjusted the sugar cubes in her other hand. After that she looked back up at her dad, and with a serious expression, she peered deeply into his concerned eyes.

Her dad was pretty touched when he heard his daughter say, "I know what I wanted all these years, Dad. But what's more important now—what I want or who needs me?"

Steffy paused briefly and then continued, "Dad that pony *needs* me! And ... well, she needs a second chance at life." The teenager was a little choked up, so she cleared her throat and added, "God sent me to Star. I just know He did!"

Her dad realized at that moment that she had made up her mind. He smiled at her and said, "Well, I guess you have yourself a pony then!"

Without more hesitation, his daughter ran back to bond with her beloved mare. Tim, Chuck, and Missy continued talking about the land that would be leased. They discussed the price and talked about relocating Star to a grassy pasture.

Steffy was happy for this time alone with her pony. The two were in their own little world. It was as if time stood still just for them. Star felt more comfortable with her new owner as the minutes passed by, and she really seemed to enjoy the sugar cubes.

The little pony was quite patient with her new girl as she let Steffy brush all the dried mud off her coat. Star's fur was matted and gummy, and it smelled quite awful. Steffy didn't mind though. She could see only her pony's true beauty. She pictured Star with a clean, velvety coat. And she pictured her with a silky-smooth mane and tail free of tangles and burs. The imaginative cowgirl could even see gorgeous, trimmed-to-perfection hooves on the ends of those crooked, little legs, because now that Star belonged to Steffy, that was exactly what she was going to look like. The young girl talked to her mare the entire time she groomed her. She wanted her pony to get to know her voice. She told Star all about the past five years and how she'd worked so hard to get her. It seemed as if Star were listening to every word Steffy said.

This cowgirl knew how crucial this bonding time was for both of them. She knew Star's first impression of her was the most important. In those moments, they were forming the foundation of their relationship. Steffy did all she knew how to do to earn her pony's trust. She knew this time would either make them or break them. She was finally able to remove all the mud from Star's coat, and then she began working very diligently to comb through her pony's mane. The teenage cowgirl was sweating as she made each tangle disappear. Finally, she was able to run her fingers through the mane, which was soft and thick. It was a beautiful jet black from the forelock halfway down her neck. The other half of her mane was pure white, and it poured into the white patches on her body. The white patches were interrupted by the black markings on her coat, making for one adorable, little black-and-white pinto pony.

Steffy stood there, admiring Star. She couldn't believe Star was hers. This wasn't just a dream anymore. She really had an equine of her very own now. She was so happy she could hardly stand it. It wasn't until she felt a cool breeze that she realized the sun was almost down.

Steffy had been standing in that muddy corral for a long time. Her boots and socks were soaked to her feet. She looked around and found a dozen curious faces studying her. The steer had been watching her as they chewed their cud. The animals seemed to have slowly migrated toward the two of them, trying to get a better look at the human, possibly wondering what in the world she was doing with *their* pony. They seemed content, though, since Star appeared quite happy with this new girl, who was giving her so much attention. It must have felt good to her to have been groomed thoroughly after not being groomed in such a long time.

Tim shook his head and smiled as he called out, "Okay, Steffer, it's time to go!"

His daughter took her pony's face in her hands one last time and said to her, "Okay, Star. I have to go now, but I promise I will be back really soon to see you again." Then she gave her mare a kiss on her fuzzy, little muzzle. After that she wrapped her arms around Star's neck and gave her a big hug. Then the pony watched her new owner climb the tall metal gate one last time that evening. Steffy looked back at her pony and said, "I love you, Starlite Mist. I have loved you for a very long time."

Tim, Chuck, and Steffy said goodbye to Missy, and the three of them drove away. The young cowgirl watched out the back window as her little pony disappeared from her sight. Then she turned back around in her seat and enjoyed the ride home. She sat there amazed by the fact that she was now the owner of a precious pinto pony.

When the ecstatic teenager arrived home, she told the rest of her family about Star. Then she called Jason, who screamed with excitement when he heard the news. Those two didn't stay on the phone long, since it was Saturday and the local horse auction in Ephrata, Pennsylvania, was swarming with hoofed animals waiting to be purchased. Jason was ready to continue his horse shopping too, and that night, he and his dad did just that.

After they hung up, Steffy called Cheryl and Darnelle. Then she called everyone in the family's address book, starting with her grandma Mama Jo. This was one of the happiest moments of her life, and she was going to share it with everyone she could think of.

Before she knew it, it was time to go to sleep. She took a shower and climbed into bed. After that she grabbed her diary and wrote in it about all that had happened that day. Lastly, she knelt down and bowed her head. "Dear God, thank you, thank you, THANK YOU, for sending me out to that farm to rescue Star. Please watch over my little mare.

The one Star needs the most Jesus, is YOU. Please help her. Thank you, Lord. In Jesus holy and precious name I pray, amen."

Early the next morning, the birds were singing and chirping as Steffy sat up in bed and rubbed her sleepy eyes. Then she got to thinking. Was it all a dream? Did she really have a pony of her own, or had she only dreamed she had a pony named Star? She was searching her tired mind for the answer when she spied her diary lying on the bed next to her. Quickly, she grabbed the worn-out notebook and scrambled through the pages until she came to the last few lines she had written. This is what she read:

Dear Diary, today is July 27th, 1985. I GOT MY FIRST PONY TODAY! I could scream! I mean, after five years of wishing on a star, I have a Star at last! She is really pretty..."

Steffy only needed to read that much, and then she said loudly, "Thank goodness! I really wasn't dreaming! I *do* have a pony!" What was that girl still doing in bed? This young pony owner had a million things to do before she could go out to see her little dumpling, and she couldn't very well do them in her pajamas. She effortlessly jumped out of bed and ran over to her dresser. Pulling her dresser drawers open, she grabbed a pair of blue jeans and a western button-down shirt. Then she grabbed her light-brown cowgirl belt that read "Steffy" on the back. She threaded it through the belt loops of her Wrangler blue jeans. The whole time she thought, *I have a pony! I have a pony! Yesterday I woke up, looking for land to lease to put a horse on, and today I have a pony! No more wishing. No more hoping. This is the real deal!*

The first thing this pet owner had to do was tend to her dogs. First, she fed them, then she gave them fresh water, and after that she took the two little ones for a walk. The beagle mix named Brownie, whom Steffy's sister Cindy rescued in the famous Blizzard of 1978, and the little white toy poodle named Tiffie, whom Steffy had gotten for her twelfth birthday, were both very happy to take a walk to the park and back. No time to play, though, for Steffy was about to burst into a million pieces if she didn't soon get to see her pony. Once they got home, she put the two little ones in the house, and then she got her guard dog Buster ready for a walk. You see, after they had lost the oldest two dogs due to old age, Steffy's dad had begun looking for a watch dog to protect the house and keep his family good and safe.

As it turned out, Darnelle had a dog that needed a good home, and he was a watch dog through and through. He had come from Darnelle's cousin's farm, the one who had the palomino the two girls had ridden. This dog was pretty protective. In fact, it took Steffy a whole year of training inside the yard just to get him ready to be walked in public. On a normal day, Steffy and this dog jogged to her old elementary school and ran around the track four times to keep her in condition for track and field. But again, this was no ordinary day; and if she didn't get to her pony in a timely manner, she was going to lose it. There was now a very special, long-awaited member of the "Steffer Tribe" just waiting to be loved and cared for. So this thirteen-year-old, horse-crazed redhead was going to get her chores done as soon as she could. She wanted to get to that pony of hers as quickly as possible.

She and Buster ended up taking a brisk walk to the school and then back again. Once home, she tended to her cat Bandit. She held him in her arms like a baby and cuddled with him, and then she fed and watered him. As he ate, his energetic owner cleaned out his litter box, and then she headed off to care for her rodents. She gave them fresh water in their bottles and a handful of food in their bowls. They all came running, knowing she would have some tasty treats for them. Steffy petted them and spoke to them softly as they ate.

Now she had to wait for someone in her family to wake up and drive her out to Woodland. The anticipation was almost unbearable. It was still quite early, and she didn't want to annoy anyone. She tried to make herself busy. First, she poured herself a bowl of cereal and ate it. No one woke up. After that, she went out to the garage, grabbed a scoopful of pigeon feed, and fed her dad's pigeons. Still, no one woke up. Now the clock read 7:30 a.m., and everyone was *still* asleep.

Steffy couldn't take it any longer. She had to get to her pony before she completely lost control. She went to Sandy's bed and watched her sleeping sister, hoping she would wake up. Sandy didn't even so much as move. Then Steffy tried to wake her by gently tugging at her pajama sleeve, still no success. The anxious thirteen-year-old stood there, not sure of what to do next.

On the one hand, she felt guilty for trying to wake up her sister at such an early hour. On the other hand, she was all but freaking out, wanting to see her pony. So she did what any impatient kid would do in her situation; she grabbed her sister's arm and began shaking it violently. "Sandy! Sandy! Wake up, please! I need to see Star *now*! Can you take me?" Steffy yelled.

Sandy was half awake, but she sat up quickly. Her eyes were still closed as she asked frantically, "Are you okay? What's wrong?" She searched for Steffy with her hands above the covers. Her little sister grabbed her hands as Steffy held back her laughter. "I'm right here. I'm really sorry to wake you, but I need to see Star. Will you take me? I've been up for hours, but no one else is up yet."

Sandy was finally able to open one of her eyes, squinting as the sunlight poured in through the bedroom window. She saw her little sister smiling and realized how funny she must have looked. The two sisters laughed and gave each other a hug. Sandy was a kind, loving soul who would do anything for anybody—or any animal, for that matter. It didn't take her long to get ready, because she knew how much this pony meant to her little sister. She was all ears and had tears of happiness welling up in her beautiful brown eyes as she listened to Steffy tell her all about Star *again*. She was so happy that Steffy's dream was finally a reality. She was proud of her baby sister for taking Star, an animal that really needed her, even though she had been waiting so long for a show horse. The more her little sister spoke of her mare, the more Sandy realized this pony needed Steffy every bit as much as Steffy needed her. She would soon see for herself just how much. Sandy finished getting dressed. Then, she and Steffy finally headed out to see Star.

As the two sisters drove up the driveway of the dairy farm, Steffy again warned tenderhearted Sandy of the condition that Star was in. She wanted to be sure her sister was prepared for what she was about to see. When they reached the farmhouse, Missy came out to greet them with the brush box. "Hey, Steffy!" she called. "Star is back over in her grassy paddock. Let me show you where that is at."

Missy introduced herself to Sandy, and she smiled at the two sisters. Then she handed Steffy the brush box and said to Sandy, "Star is one lucky little pony. We moved her to the steer pasture the day before we were going to put her down. That way she could indulge in some grain one last time and die happy, with a full belly. The little cutie loves to eat. So we thought we'd give her one last good meal. The next thing we know, Steffy shows up and wants to rescue her. Pretty good timing for that little mare, I'd say. Anyway, we put her back in her paddock. It's right over there." She pointed to a fenced-in grassy area not too far away. "Just let yourself in through the gate and latch it securely once you're through. If you need me, I will be working in the yard." She walked back toward the house, and the two siblings headed to the grassy paddock.

There stood Steffy's pony. The teenage cowgirl smiled big and stated, "There she is! That's my pony, Star!" Now, Sandy may not have been as educated about horses and ponies as Steffy, but it didn't take an equine specialist to realize that this unfortunate creature needed medical attention—and she needed it as soon as possible.

Sandy stood there, her jaw dropping in disbelief, as she scanned every inch of Star's body. When her eyes reached the pony's hooves, the first words that came out of her mouth were, "Steffy, how can I help her?"

Her little sister answered, "I don't really know where to start. I know the veterinarian I want to use, but I think we better find a blacksmith to trim those long hooves first."

Sandy replied with heartfelt concern, "Steffy, do whatever you need to do here quickly, because we need to find someone to trim those hooves right away!"

Steffy answered, "Okay." She slowly walked over to her pony. "Hey girl, how are you? I missed you so much. I couldn't wait to get here and see you again." As she brushed her mare, she spoke in a soft voice. She told her new pony all about how she had called dozens of people and told them all about her. Steffy kept speaking as she held the hoof pick up to Star's nostrils to introduce it to her, just as she had with the brush the day before. She gently ran it along Star's face, across her neck, and down her front right leg. She held her pony's leg in her left hand and then ran her hand down it. Finally, she squeezed the tendon at Star's pastern and tugged gently on the hair of the fetlock. Her pony's eyes widened, showing she was clearly scared.

Nervously, Star brought her hoof up off the ground for just a split second. She wasn't able to balance herself on her other three legs very well due to the shape her hooves were in. However, her owner was able to see enough of the hoof to realize Star was in worse shape than she had thought. The little pony quickly pulled her leg away from her new owner. Then she started moving sideways and snorting. She was shaking. The event clearly made her unhappy. When Steffy tried to get her other front hoof up off the ground, Star pinned her ears back. Steffy knew what *that* meant, so she stopped before she got bit. Star calmed down as Steffy petted her neck and face. Then she gave her pony a hug and a kiss.

After seeing the bottom of that hoof, Steffy was very concerned. She said to her pony, "Sorry I have to leave you so soon, girl. I need to get you some help. I love you." Steffy gathered up the brush box and headed back to her sister.

When she got back to Sandy, she had a look of concern. She tapped her thigh nervously, and then with her eyes wide and her face pale, she said, "Sandy, you are right. Star needs a blacksmith right now!"

The two sisters walked toward Sandy's car. The eldest watched the youngest put the brush box up against the side of the house. They both waved goodbye to Missy, who was pulling weeds on the other side of the lawn. Missy saw them and waved back, smiling. Then Steffy said, "Sandy, Star's hooves are so weird. I mean, not only are they long from overgrowth and wrinkled from the founder, but when I saw the bottom of her hoof, I almost freaked."

Sandy asked, "What did it look like?" With a questioning look, she added, "And what is it *supposed* to look like?"

Steffy put her right hand up and cupped it, resembling a shallow letter *C*. "Okay, pretend this is the bottom of a healthy hoof. It's kind of dished in like this, and the edges of it are flat." Her sister nodded in understanding. "Well," she continued, "Star's hoof didn't have an edge at all. The edges of her hoof have grown inward and overlapped the dished-in part. I couldn't get under the overlapped 'flaps' to clean the inside of the hoof. It was just awful. I can't believe this. She must be in terrible pain, Sandy. Not to mention the disease."

Her sister asked, "Disease? What do you mean?"

"Well, if the hooves are all overgrown and overlapping the inside of themselves, then all the manure and mud are trapped in those hooves. It is keeping the hooves from getting the oxygen they need to stay healthy. The hooves literally rot. This disease is called 'thrush.' I have read about this kind of thing. It could kill her, Sandy!"

"Okay then, the first thing we need to do is pray! Star needs God. She cannot get better without Him." Just before the two sisters reached a stop sign at the end of the road, there was a little corner restaurant on the right-hand side. They pulled into the parking lot, and Sandy shut the car off. Then she reached for Steffy's hands and held them in her own. She and Steffy closed their eyes and bowed their heads.

Sandy prayed aloud, "Dear Lord, please help Star. Please heal her little feet. We ask that You will help us find a good blacksmith for her. Thank You. In Jesus' name, we pray, amen."

Steffy added, "Amen!"

Sandy looked over at the restaurant and said, "Hey, maybe someone in here can tell us where to find a good blacksmith." The two of them got out of the car and walked inside, Sandy leading the way. Once they entered, she said loudly, "Excuse me, does anyone here know of a good blacksmith?"

The restaurant attendant was very friendly, and he gave them the name of a well-respected blacksmith/horse trainer. Then Sandy asked the nice man for a phone and a phonebook. He kindly gave her both. She immediately looked up the blacksmith's name. After that, she got on the phone and dialed the number.

The phone rang a couple of times, and a man answered. "Hello?"

Sandy began, "Hello, my name is Sandy. I am looking for a man by the name of Parry. My little sister has a pony that really needs his help." The man told her she was talking to Parry, so she went into full detail about Star's condition. Without hesitation the concerned man scheduled an appointment. It would be three days from then. It was the first available opening he had. Sandy thanked him and the restaurant attendant. After that, she hugged her little sister. Then they left.

When they reached the car, they got in, buckled up, and Sandy began to drive. Steffy said, as a tear came to her eye, "Thanks. I don't know what I'd do without you." Sandy smiled at her little sister, and they headed home.

★ CHAPTER 6 ★

𝕰𝕺 *Best Friends* 𝕺𝕰

THAT NIGHT STEFFY had her best friend, Cheryl, over to spend the night with her in the tree house; better known as the "Girls Hideaway Club." It wasn't actually in a tree; it was more like a miniature house on stilts. It was as high as the trees in the backyard, and it had a long set of wooden stairs and a little front porch with a railing. It had a porch light on the outside, a single light inside, and an outlet for electricity. The little house had two windows and was fully insulated. The walls were covered in medium-brown paneling, and the ceiling was white. It had two little built-in shelves in the back wall. The clubhouse had dark-orange tile on the floor, and it was fully furnished with sleeping bags, pillows, and a tiny TV. There was a cooler, too, that Steffy kept filled with ice and pop, kind of like a little mini fridge.

Every kid in town thought the tree house was awesome, and Steffy and her sisters were very thankful their dad had built it for them. This teenage Christian used it to witness her faith in Jesus Christ. She held sleepovers up there throughout the summer weeks, and on the weekends, she invited two to three girls over at a time. They watched TV, did each other's hair, ate snacks, and drank pop. Then if the next day wasn't Sunday, they slept in, but if the next day *was* Sunday, she and Sandy loaded the kids up in Sandy's car and took them to church.

Word spread around the neighborhood about the activity at the Girls Hideaway Club, and everyone wanted to hang out there. Before she knew it, Steffy was a witnessing machine. Sometimes when it was just the two of them, Steffy and Cheryl pretended this tree house was their apartment. Of course, they had to imagine it was twenty times larger than its size, for it was pretty small. But they had a great time pretending to be out on their own, all grown up.

It was now Saturday, and the best friends had a sleepover of two, just them. They stayed up most of the night, writing down things Steffy would need for Star. Cheryl helped her best friend make a list of everyone in her family. Then she created a schedule for them. This consisted of days they would take turns driving Steffy to the barn. The girls planned, wrote, and organized for hours. Finally, they drifted off to sleep, with Steffy's cat lying between them and pens and notebooks still in hand.

The next morning the giddy teenagers began their busy day. First, they got dressed, did Steffy's chores, and finally waited on Sandy. It was Sunday, and even before her long-awaited pony visit, Steffy couldn't wait to go to church and serve the Lord. After all, if it wasn't for Him, she never would have gotten that little mare. She was excited to go to church and praise Him. That teenager couldn't wait to sing to God and thank Him with all her might. Finally, Sandy was ready, and the three were on their way.

As on any Sunday morning, Sandy first drove around to all the people on her list and picked up as many kids as her Chevelle could hold. When the car was good and full, they headed to church. Once inside, they greeted all their church friends and went downstairs to their Sunday school classes. After Sunday school was over, everyone went upstairs to the sanctuary and seated themselves in the pews. The opportunity came for Steffy to give a praise report, and she was all smiles as she told the church congregation the wonderful news about Star. Everyone was so happy for her. Steffy thought that morning seemed to be as perfect as could be.

Sandy promised the girls that she would take them to see Star later that afternoon. So, after church the two best friends rode their bikes to Cheryl's house to start Cheryl's chores. After they finished, they called Sandy. Steffy asked her sister to grab her camera. She wanted to take pictures of her pony. Sandy grabbed the camera and picked up the girls; then the three of them headed to Woodland. Talking nonstop for the entire drive, they passed the time quickly. When they reached the small town, Steffy clenched her fists tightly. Then she squeezed her eyes shut and said excitedly, "We are almost there."

Cheryl quickly said, "Oh my gosh. I can't believe I am about to meet your pony." Then she happily tapped her feet on the floorboard superfast, imitating the sound of a drumroll.

The girls wished they could put the car into turbo speed to get there faster. Once they reached the farm, it seemed like it took forever for them to drive up the long driveway. As soon as Sandy parked the car, the girls took off out of it as quickly as possible. Steffy ran up to the house and grabbed the brush box from the side of the house, and Cheryl followed her toward the grassy paddock, where Star stood. Now there was one thing about Cheryl a person could always count on, and that was the plain, simple fact that she spoke her mind. As anyone who knows her can tell you, if you want an honest opinion, you will get one from Cheryl. And if she doesn't speak it with her mouth, the look on her face will say it all.

So when her green eyes followed her best friend's pointed finger to the small, sickly looking mare, her bright smile quickly faded into a confused frown. And her nose wrinkled up like a prune. If that wasn't bad enough, just to be sure one could tell what she was thinking, Cheryl's mouth puckered up as if she had been sucking on a lemon … a very sour one. "No way," was all she could say. With her head slowly moving from side to side, she couldn't stop the same two words from slipping out of her mouth. "No way," she repeated in a whisper.

A bit more than annoyed, Steffy obnoxiously said, "Yes way." Then she collected herself and took in a deep breath. Optimistically and trying very hard to smile, she added, "That's her! My pony, Star! My dream-come true."

Once again Steffy was lost for a moment in her new little world, the world where she could envision Star's beauty beyond her pain. She was in that place where she could see Star's courage beyond her fear, where she could exist for brief periods of time and see Star through another pair of eyes. The hopeful teenager could sense her pony's strength in those moments, her fight. She could almost feel that energy radiating off Starlite Mist and onto herself. She could see it, and in time, everyone else would be able to see it too.

Steffy said with hope in her voice, "I know she needs a lot of help. But I also know that I can help her. I can help her like people help ponies in equine rescues."

Cheryl lovingly interrupted. "Stef," she said as she looked compassionately into her best friend's eyes, "I don't want to be mean or anything, but this is not some pigeon with a broken wing here." She looked at Star, and then she looked back at Steffy, and then said, "This is a sick little pony with some major problems. Are you even sure you want to attempt this one?" Cheryl's green eyes pierced her best friend's blue eyes, which were now filling with great, big tears.

"Cheryl!" Steffy said in a loud voice. "*This* is the pony God wants me to have. Don't you see? He sent me to her." Unable to hold the tears back, she had no choice but to let them roll down her cheeks. "Now stop talking like that! She can hear you!" The emotional equestrian was finally able to lower her voice and then she said, "I am supposed to give this mare a second chance at life. I can do it. I know I can. With God *all* things are possible."

Cheryl's look of concern finally turned into one of hope. She could see the determination in her best friend's face. She recognized it. She had seen it before. This teenager knew Steffy believed every word coming out of her mouth. And now Cheryl was beginning to believe those words as well. She gave her best friend a hug, and the two girls walked over to the precious pony.

Sandy called, "I will be back to pick you up in two hours, okay?"

Steffy yelled back, "Okay!" The girls waved goodbye to her, and finally Steffy introduced her little mare to her best friend.

"Hi there, girl," Cheryl said softly as she rubbed Star's fuzzy face. "She is *so cute!*"

Steffy gave Cheryl some sugar cubes to give to her. Missy had stocked the brush box with them. This time of connection made Steffy happy. The more time Cheryl spent with those two on that farm, the more confidence she had in them. She became more hopeful that Steffy really was going to get that little pony stronger and better. She knew her best friend well enough to know she was either going to rehabilitate that pony or put herself in the hospital trying.

Cheryl knew all the stories about how Steffy, with her dad's help, had spent her childhood rehabilitating pigeons with wounded wings, rescuing wild baby birds, and training each of her dogs. She'd heard the story of how Steffy had strived year after year, trying to earn a horse—not to mention the fact that she had just spent her entire seventh-grade year watching her best friend struggle to get a perfect report card so she could make that dream a reality. She knew what Steffy was capable of doing. Win, lose, or draw, that pony was going to be loved *a lot* and taken care of to the best of Steffy's ability.

The girls enjoyed every minute of those two hours with Star. They decided to take pictures before the sun went down. Steffy gave Cheryl her camera. Star was standing right next to the hay manger, so Steffy decided to sit on it to be at her pony's eye level. Then she put her right hand on Star's right cheek and gently pulled her little mare's face up next to her own. Once they were cheek to cheek, Cheryl said, "Okay! Say *cheeeeeeeeeese!*"

Star's ears perked forward, and she looked dead center, straight at the camera. Turns out, she was quite photogenic. Who would have guessed? Steffy gave a big ear-to-ear smile, and Cheryl snapped the picture. Then she held the camera steady for a couple of seconds to make sure the shot had taken.

"Hey! That was our very first picture," Steffy said, still smiling.

Cheryl looked proud, and with a smile she said, "Yep! And I took it." The two girls giggled while Star just stared at them.

"I'm going to get a picture of those hooves. Nobody is going to believe this. We need proof," Cheryl said as she got a close-up picture of Star's overgrown hooves. Steffy agreed; before and after pictures of those things would be priceless.

Soon the sun began to fade, and the girls heard the familiar rumble of Sandy's car pulling up into the driveway. They gathered the grooming supplies and put them in the brush box. Then the two BFFs gave Star plenty of hugs and kisses to hold her over until the next day.

After letting themselves out of the pasture and securing the latch behind them, they placed the brush box next to the farmhouse. Then the two teenagers walked side by side to the car, smiling the entire time. They climbed into the back seat of Sandy's car together. At the same time they turned around to look at the cute, little pony from the back window. The girls waved and simultaneously said, "Bye, Star!" After that, they turned to each other and said, "Jinx! You owe me a Cherry Coke!" Giggling down the road, the two best friends told Sandy all about their visit with Star.

★ CHAPTER 7 ★

 *Star's Angel*

THE NEXT TWO days came and went, and Cheryl's schedule came in handy. Between Steffy's parents and her two sisters, the four drivers divvied up their weeks and agreed on who would drive Steffy to the farm and who would go back to get her. Steffy was so grateful for her family. Their support and effort were essential. Without them she would have had no way to go to the farm to see Star.

Before she knew it, the big day arrived to meet Parry, the blacksmith. Both Sandy and Cindy went to take their little sister to Woodland. Cindy hadn't yet seen Star, and her work schedule finally enabled her to do so. The three sisters eagerly headed to the dairy farm together.

Sandy, who solely relied on the Lord, suggested that they pray before they started the commute. She knew that "…where two or three are gathered in [His] name, [He] is in the midst of them." Matthew 18:20 NKJV. So the three sisters prayed an earnest prayer, thanking God for giving Star a second chance at life. They all asked God to work through Parry's hands as he worked on Star's disfigured and overgrown hooves. Steffy was optimistic, and she imagined what Star might look like in a few months after being worked on.

This thought made her smile inside. Little did she know that the work she was about to get involved in was going to be unbelievably challenging. She was about to find out that everything she had learned regarding horses and ponies over the last five years was about to be applied to her life right here, right now—everything she had learned up until this point and so much more.

Sandy announced to Steffy, "Dad told me this morning that he talked to Missy. She told him she moved Star to the pasture next to the hayfield. Dad also called the blacksmith and gave him directions on how to get there. See?" Sandy pointed over to a pasture just past the farmhouse. "It is right over there where that big red barn is."

The young cowgirl's eyes lit up, and a big smile came across her face. There appeared to be a little over five acres of lush grassy land, and there was a big red barn sitting in the middle of it.

There was also a wooded area beyond the barn and a crystal-clear creek running through the back of it. Star shared this piece of land with ten adorable, little calves, who instantly adopted the black-and-white pony as their surrogate mom. Star seemed to accept this new responsibility without hesitation, and she instantly became the leader of the herd.

Missy was waiting for them at the pasture's entrance. She sat in her truck with a smile. The three sisters parked the car and greeted her. Cindy hadn't yet met her, so she politely introduced herself. Missy was happy to meet her as well. After introductions, the property owner began to explain all the rules of this new pasture and what she expected from Steffy. She showed her how to open and close the gate properly.

In addition, she stressed how crucial it was for her to always close the gate behind her and fasten it securely every time she went through it. This step would ensure the safety of the calves as well as Star by keeping them from accidentally getting out. She proceeded to tell her when feeding time would be for Star and discussed details of that nature. When she finished, Missy said goodbye to Steffy and her sisters, and she drove back to her house.

Sandy and Cindy watched as their little sister let herself in through the rusted metal gate and secured the latch behind her. All ten little calves ran up to her in hopes of getting something to eat. Being a few hours away from feeding time, they had to settle for hugs and a back scratching instead. The calves seemed satisfied with that, and then they scattered off a few at a time back into the grassy field. Steffy reached into her pocket and pulled out a couple of fresh, sweet, crunchy carrots.

Star made her way over to her owner, tripping over her long hooves in the process. She was a little skeptical of Sandy and Cindy. But she must have sensed Steffy's trust. After a few minutes, she decided to move a little closer to her owner. Besides, the smell of those juicy carrots was simply too irresistible, and the drive to get to them outweighed any fear she may have had.

Cindy's eyes fixed on Star's hooves. She stared at them for a while. Then she looked at Steffy and said with heartfelt concern, "What happened to her poor feet?" She added, "This blacksmith guy is going to fix those, right?"

Steffy smiled and answered, "Yep! He is going to fix her up as good as new. You'll see."

Cindy nodded and said, "Good. That looks very painful. How often does a pony need its feet trimmed?"

Her little sister answered, "A horse or pony usually needs their hooves trimmed every month to month and a half. This little girl must have gone *years* without hoof care."

"Poor thing," Cindy said. "I am really glad she has you now, Steffy." Cindy gave her little sister a big smile, and Steffy smiled back.

After that Steffy patted Star's furry nose. Then she let her pony take each carrot from her hand. She put her freckled face next Star's face and breathed into her tiny nostrils. Sandy and Cindy both seemed a little grossed out and somewhat confused by this. Then Steffy explained, "This is how horses and ponies greet each other. It's kind of like when people shake hands or give each other a high five." She giggled at her sisters' expressions.

The look on Sandy's face went from a my-baby-sister-is-nuts look to a that-kind-of-makes-sense expression. As for Cindy, well, she still looked grossed out and confused. Their little sister knew though. She was the animal lover in the family. No one could really comprehend her tactics unless they were as crazy about animals as she was. Their dad was pretty much the only other family member who could come close to understanding her.

Steffy wanted in the worst way to have the same close bond with her pony that the children had with their horses in the books she had read. She remembered reading somewhere, "For every horse there is one true leader, one rider that the animal would lay down his life for." That was the type of bond she wanted to create with Star. She didn't want Star just to have a pony to add to her collection of pets. She didn't want to put her on a shelf like a trophy, so to speak. She dreamed of having Star for a very long time. She'd worked so hard to earn her. Now the young girl's heart was full of compassion and empathy. She wanted to give her little mare a good quality of life. She wanted to love her until her pony grew old and passed away from old age. In addition, she wanted not only to rehabilitate Star physically, but she also wanted to make her whole again emotionally.

This horse-crazed teenager wanted to get close enough to her mare to be able to grab a hold of her little heart and slowly and gently mend it back together again, with one act of love at a time. She wanted their relationship to mean something. She wanted them to develop an inseparable, lifelong bond. In fact, that young cowgirl wasn't going to settle for anything less.

A few minutes passed, and the three girls noticed an old white pickup truck, with a big metal chest in the bed, appear from down the road. It pulled up and parked behind Sandy's car. A man with dark-brown hair, brown eyes, and a medium height emerged from the truck. He walked around to the front of Sandy's car and said with a smile, "Hi. I'm Parry, the blacksmith." He took turns shaking hands with the three girls; each introduced herself with a smile.

When it was Steffy's turn, the proud pony owner added, wrapping her arm around her mare's soft neck, "And this is my pony, Star."

Parry smiled and said as he let himself into the pasture, "Star! Well, it is very nice to meet you, girl. Let's get those hooves looked at, shall we?" Then he began to study Star's hooves and legs. He looked very closely as he wrinkled his forehead and raised his left eyebrow higher than the right one. He walked slowly around to the right side of Star. Then he walked back around to the left side, keeping his eyes fixed on her lower extremities.

Horses and ponies were Parry's life. Trimming, shaping, repairing, and maintaining their hooves were his art. He seemed to be dissatisfied with merely looking at the pony's hooves. He needed to be able to handle them. He wanted to know exactly what he was dealing with here. First, the gentle man began speaking to Star in a soft, calm voice. He told her his name and then began explaining to her why he was there. Star's eyes watched him intensely. She knew he was speaking to her, and she seemed to be interested in what he was saying. He continued talking as he began walking closer to her. He held out his hand, and Star smelled it. He gently patted her face and her neck.

Star seemed to enjoy his soothing voice and gentle touch. She didn't seem to mind him petting her. Then he ran his hands from the top of each leg down to the hoof. After that he felt the outline of each of Star's leg muscles, tendons, ligaments, and bones. He pressed firmly with his fingers and his thumbs. He didn't want to miss anything. When he finished his assessment, he stepped away from her. Then he studied her legs and feet once more, again from a distance.

He scratched his head, and a look of sincere concern came over his face. This made the young cowgirl uneasy. She somehow knew the look he was giving meant business. She wasn't sure whether she wanted to hear what he had to say. She had a feeling it was bad.

Her eyes welled up with huge crocodile tears before she had the chance to fight them back as she heard him say, "I have to be honest with you, Steffy. If I were any other blacksmith, I would call a vet and have this poor animal put out of her misery."

Steffy felt her stomach turn to knots. *Put my pony down? No way,* she thought. *Why would God bring me and Star together just to turn around and let her life end?* She didn't believe God would want something like that to happen. But here was a man who by law could have Star taken and put to sleep humanely for her own sake.

She started to feel scared. Then she started to feel sick. Just the thought of losing her little mare was enough to make her nauseous. With tears in her eyes, she held her belly with one hand and took in a long, deep breath. Looking deeply into Parry's concerned eyes, Steffy gave him a please-don't-have-her-taken-away-from-me look. Then the look on his face changed from concern for the unhealthy pony to compassion for the brokenhearted girl.

He cleared his throat and said, "Then again, I am not just any blacksmith. I can see that you really love this pony." He shifted his eyes once again in Star's direction and added, "I'll tell you what. If you want to put this pony out of her misery, I will help you do that. But if you want to try to put all her missing pieces back together again, I'm willing to help you do that too."

At that moment, it seemed as if Steffy's heart leaped. She felt a release from the fear she was feeling, and she let out a sigh of relief.

Instantly, Steffy's stomach wasn't in knots anymore, and the tears she had been trying to fight back weren't building up like they had been. Looks of hope and gratitude came across her face. She pulled Star's halter gently toward her. Then she put her pony's fuzzy muzzle in her hands and squatted down. With her face resting on Star's, she kissed her pony's soft nose. Then she slowly stood up.

Looking at the blacksmith, she replied, "I know she is in really bad shape, but this pony needs me to help her. She deserves that much. That's why God put us here, you and me, to give her a second chance at life." The teenager wiped her runny nose and tear-stained cheeks with the back of her hand. Then she sniffed a couple of times.

"Well then," Parry said. "I think you are doing the right thing." The girl's face lit up. "But remember this," he added quickly. "What we will need to do for her is going to take a lot of hard work, complete dedication, and a whole lot of time and patience. And Steffy," he added with a softer tone in his voice, "there is a chance she might not make it. And if she does make it, she will never be able to carry more than her own weight." He paused for a moment and then he continued, "Which means, you will never be able to ride her."

Steffy nodded to show she understood what he was saying. Before he got started, Parry had Steffy run her hands along Star's legs. He explained to her everything she was touching. He told her what healthy, straight pony legs looked and felt like as opposed to what Star's unhealthy, crooked legs looked and felt like.

The teenager was beginning to understand just how serious Star's condition really was. She appreciated that Parry had taken the time to explain the situation to her. The caring cowboy smiled at the little red-haired, horse-crazed girl and said, "Well, if we wanna get her better, I need to get to work on those hooves."

He went to his truck and brought back with him a lead rope and his hoof-trimming equipment. He handed Steffy the rope and instructed her to attach it to Star's halter. Steffy did as Parry said. Star saw and smelled the equipment, and she began to get anxious. Parry warned Steffy that she would have to use all her strength to handle her pony.

Sandy and Cindy watched with curiosity from the safety of the opposite side the fence. Parry began speaking to Star softly and petting her. He ran his hand down her front leg again, this time squeezing her tendon and pulling on her fetlock. The pony knew he was asking her for her hoof, and she knew he was going to use those scary tools to try to trim it. She also knew the procedure was going to be very painful. Needless to say, when Parry finally picked up her hoof, Star pulled her head around so fast that most of the lead rope slipped out of Steffy's hands. And without any hesitation, the frightened pony bit Parry right smack-dab square in the pants. Steffy's jaw dropped as she quickly gathered the lead rope and held it tighter. She apologized with, "Sorry 'bout that! Are you okay?" Cindy and Sandy giggled quietly to themselves. Their little sister, on the other hand, was quite embarrassed by her pony's aggressive behavior.

Parry nodded, and then tried a second time to pull Star's hoof up off the ground. Star was even more nervous than before, and at first, she stepped sideways. Then she reared straight up on her hind legs like horses do in movies. This caused the little mare even more pain, so she whipped her head around. With her ears pinned back, her stained teeth bared, and her eyes closed tightly, she took another bite. But it was Steffy's bottom she bit this time.

The shocked teenager jumped and yelled, "Ouch!"

Parry reached for the lead rope and patiently said, "Here, let me take her."

Steffy handed the rope to Parry and grabbed the seat of her pants. After that, she hobbled over to her sisters and turned around to show them her injury. They both examined her hind quarters as she asked, "Am I bleeding?"

Her sisters shook their heads at the same time. They had to work hard at holding back their laughter. As much as they felt bad that Steffy and Parry were experiencing pain, they found the entire scenario completely hilarious.

Parry said to Steffy, handing her the lead rope once more, "Are you all right?" She nodded and took the rope. "Okay, we need reinforcement," he said. Then he looked around and spotted something they could use. He pointed to a strong maple tree not far from where they were standing. He said, "Go ahead and tie her up to that tree over there."

Steffy tied Star securely to the tree, with the lead rope tied in a cowboy knot. Parry collected his supplies and followed them over, while Sandy and Cindy went to sit in Sandy's car to wait.

Before he got started, Parry introduced Star to the equipment. The little pony became nervous from the familiar smell of it. The wise man knew this, so he took it slow and easy. When Star calmed down, he stopped and petted her. Finally, he began working on her hooves.

The little pony didn't like the procedure. First, she tried to back up; then she tried to rear up. But the strong tree held her well, and she was unable to succeed. Next, she tried to bite her owner, but Steffy was ready this time, and she pushed Star's mouth away from her. After that, her pony tried to bite the blacksmith, but the careful redhead was ready for that too. She quickly maneuvered her pony's face away from Parry's body.

Before long the three of them were dripping with sweat. Wrestling with Star wasn't an easy feat, but the two determined humans didn't stop until the job was finished. And when they were finally done, all three were completely exhausted.

Parry said between breaths, "Well, that's all I can do for today. I took a lot of hoof off, but I still have a lot of work to do with the old gal." He patted Star gently on the neck and said, "It looks to me like I better come out at least every two weeks. I am going to need to get her feet to a more normal length." He wiped the sweat off his face with the bottom of his T-shirt and added, "If I do it now all at once, she'll go lame. We will have to take it nice and slow. We want to keep her pain to a minimum."

Steffy wiped the sweat off her face with the backs of her hands as she listened to Parry speak. He continued, "In the meantime, you'll have to start working with her. Even though she will never be able to be ridden, you still need to teach her manners and get her down to a healthy weight. The excess fat she is carrying is causing her more pain than we know." Then he said, "Go ahead. Take her lead rope off her and let her go. She put up with enough from us for one day."

Star received a hug and a kiss from her owner as Steffy removed the lead rope. Star slowly began to walk away with a limp. Steffy could tell her feet were tender. After all, it was the first trim she'd had in who knows how long. However, she noticed her pony didn't have to struggle as much to walk, *and* she was no longer tripping over her hooves.

Star just needed to get used to walking with shorter hooves. The exhausted equestrian was really excited. This was a big step for her new pony (no pun intended). Star was on her way to a new life. It was their first hurdle conquered in their race toward the finish line, and Steffy felt good about it. Before Parry left that day, he told Steffy what they needed to start doing for Star.

"I have a lot to teach you, so pay close attention to everything I say," he said.

The teenager answered, "Yes, sir."

"First, have you ever lunged a horse before?"

"No. I have only read about it and watched other people do it. But I know I can do it if you teach me. I'm a quick learner, and I am good with animals."

Parry looked at her with a serious expression. "You will have to be. This mare needs ground work, and a lot of it. Ground work is going to play a big role in saving her life." Then he continued, "You need to handle her every chance you get. She needs to be able to sense your love for her. There is a long road ahead of you two, and Star needs you to show her the way. Do you understand?"

Steffy nodded. She knew Parry was very serious, so she listened very carefully to him.

"First, you will need a long lunge line and a long whip," he said. Steffy looked concerned. Parry continued, "Don't worry. You won't use the whip *on* her. You will only need to tap the ground behind her hind hooves. You will do this to get her to go from a standing position to a walk, from a walk to a trot, and possibly later on, from a trot to a canter. But for now, standing to a walk and a walk to a trot will be fine. You will need to make sure that you introduce her to every bit of the new equipment that you get. Let her smell it. Run it along her face and neck, then her body and legs. Finally, run the equipment across her belly and down her tail."

Parry continued, "Next, you will need to clip the end of the lunge line onto her halter and hold the rest of it in your hands like this." He collected Star's lead rope in a circular fashion, and then he gripped it in the middle and said, "Always hold the lunge line this way, never in the shape of a lasso. Otherwise, if your mare decided to take off, the line would tighten up around your hand, and you could get caught up in it."

He had a serious look on his face, and Steffy listened to him intentionally. She had read about people who got caught up and dragged by horses. Some people had serious injuries, and others have even died from the experience. She knew that was something she would have to be extra careful about.

Parry said, "You must walk your pony in a circle, allowing the lunge line to get a little longer with every circle you make. If she doesn't want to walk the circle around you, hit the ground behind her with the whip. In case she has ever been abused in the past, we want her to understand and not be afraid of any of the equipment. We want her to grow to trust you and love you. I don't believe in breaking a horse's spirit down. I believe in gaining a horse's trust so he or she can become trainable."

Steffy was so happy in that moment. She knew Parry had been sent there by God Himself. In the beginning, she'd only expected a blacksmith, but with God in the middle of this whole thing, He'd made sure He supplied a very gentle blacksmith, who was also an exceptional trainer.

Parry went on to tell Steffy that her pony may want to stop in the middle of lunging and might walk up to her. If this happened, Steffy would need to take Star back out to where she was walking, show her the whip, and make a clicking sound with her mouth. If her pony continued to walk up to her, Steffy needed to push her away. He told her she needed to be very patient, and Star should eventually give up and obey her commands.

"You must be very consistent," he said. "I will only be here once every couple of weeks to guide you. The rest is up to you. Are you up to it?"

Steffy answered quickly, "Oh yes! I can do it."

Parry added, "Now don't let her get away with anything. Correct her when she gets too feisty, and whatever you do, if she tries to run off while you are lunging her, don't let her. She's going to test you to see what she can get away with, so you have to be ready. The last thing you want is for that mare to think she is in charge. Got it?"

Steffy answered, "Got it!" She gave him a big smile.

"Good. Then I will see you two weeks from today, same time."

Steffy dug into her front pocket and pulled out a wrinkled ten-dollar bill. "Thanks for not charging much. Thanks for everything! See you in two weeks."

He smiled at her, grabbed his tools, and headed for his truck. Then he threw his tools into the metal chest, waved goodbye, and left.

Steffy made her way to Sandy's car. She stopped briefly, turned around, and blew Star a kiss. After that she called out to her, "Goodbye, girl! I'll see you tomorrow!" All the way home, Steffy thanked God for Star. And now that this blacksmith/trainer had been added into the equation of Star's life, Steffy felt as though her little mare really did have a chance to live again. She knew God had led her every footstep straight to Parry, Star's angel.

★ CHAPTER 8 ★

ᘓᕲ *Training from the Ground Up* ᕲᘔ

THAT WEEK WAS the beginning of Star's ground work. The enthusiastic teenager was excited. It was a beautiful summer day, just perfect for training her pony. Sharon arrived home from work ready to help her daughter with anything she needed regarding this training. Steffy stuffed her pockets full of carrots to give to her little mare. Then her mom drove her to the only local tack shop around, the famous Al-Bar Ranch. This amazing tack shop was owned and operated by some of the nicest residents of Mishawaka, Indiana. It was beautiful and spacious inside, and packed full of everything and anything an equestrian and equine could ever need or want.

Steffy loved that place. For years her parents had taken her there just to allow her to dream and hope. Her dad always said, "If you don't have hope, you don't have anything." He had bought lead ropes from Al-Bar Ranch for his daughter to use as leashes for their guard dog, Buster. That dog needed a super-strong leash, and using a lead rope helped Steffy feel one step closer to owning a horse. To help Steffy keep her hope, her parents had taken her to Al-Bar Ranch on her eleventh and twelfth birthdays.

While their little cowgirl-wanna-be was busy looking around, her dad had asked the owners of the tack shop to present Steffy with an award that he had made up at the local trophy shop. On her eleventh birthday, the owners presented Steffy with a plaque with a horse face engraved on it. It read, "To our #1 Animal Lover STEFANIE HACKER, Happy Birthday, from Al-Bar Ranch." On Steffy's twelfth birthday, the wonderful owners presented Steffy with a trophy that had a horse on top of it. It read, "Steffy Hacker #1 Animal Lover."

The awards weren't a horse, but Steffy thought she would bubble over with happiness when she was presented with them. Steffy's dad was always full of surprises, and people seemed to enjoy playing along. The owners of Al-Bar Ranch knew of Steffy's dreams to own a horse someday, and they were thrilled to be part of the "happy" in her birthdays.

Now this same girl was walking through the same door, only she wasn't there to purchase a lead rope for her dog—no, sir. She was there to purchase lunging equipment for her very own pony. She was so excited to tell the staff about Star, and they were all smiles to hear about her. That horse-crazed teenager loved the smell of leather in that tack shop. In addition, she liked the sound of metal on metal, when two bits hit each other, as one of the owners arranged two bridles down the aisle. It was like music to her ears. This was her kind of place, especially since she was now an official pony owner.

The mother-daughter duo explained to the clerk behind the counter that they were in need of lunging equipment. They mentioned that they didn't need anything fancy, just the most affordable equipment they had in stock. The man asked them to follow him and said there was a large selection to choose from, and he was right. Steffy looked the selection over and picked out the least-expensive whip and lunge line. As any horse person will tell you, there is no such thing as cheap horse equipment, but some of it is more affordable than others.

She held the price tags up to her mom and said, "These are the cheapest they have."

Her mom saw the prices and shrugged. "Okay, well, you need it, so we'll take it," her mom said. "Just don't mention any prices to your dad unless he asks." Steffy nodded in agreement, and they smiled at each other. After that, the two thanked the good people at the tack shop. Everyone there told Steffy how happy they were for her. They all wished her luck with her training. Steffy and her mom bought the supplies and left. They discussed Star's training during the entire one-hour drive from Al-Bar Ranch in Mishawaka to Star's barn in Woodland.

When they finally arrived, Steffy gathered the whip and the lunge line. Then she adjusted the carrots in her pockets. After that she got out of the car. As she headed for the gate, she could hear the sound of little hooves beating on the ground. The calves and her pony were all on their way to greet her.

Steffy's mom called, "I will be back in three hours. Will that give you enough time?" Sharon stood in the doorway of the car, with her right knee on the driver's seat and her left arm resting on top of the car door.

Steffy called back to her mom, "Yeah that should give us enough time. Thanks for everything, Mom! I love you!"

Her mom smiled as she called back, "I love you too, honey!" Then she slipped into her car and drove away. With one hand out the window, she waved goodbye until she was out of sight. Steffy waved back, thankful for such a loving mom and for her new training supplies.

She reached across the fence and carefully placed the equipment on the ground. Then she let herself into the beautiful pasture and secured the latch behind her. She greeted all the baby cows and patted them. When they had their fill of attention, they all scattered away, and Star walked up to her new owner. She buried her nose into her girl's side, tickling her. The little pony's nostrils flared, and she made some funny noises as she searched for the sweet treats. She could smell them deep inside those jacket pockets.

Steffy laughed as she pulled the carrots out and said, "Here, girl. You sure do like to eat!" The chubby pony munched happily on the vegetables. Then she bobbed her head up and down as if to say, *You bet I do!*

The young cowgirl patted Star's face and giggled. Her pony was so stinkin' cute, she could hardly stand it. After she snuggled her hairy girl for fifteen minutes or so, Steffy decided she had better get started with their training. She held the lunge line and the whip out in front of her pony, allowing Star to smell them. Then Steffy ran them gently across Star's face and then all over her fuzzy body, just as Parry had instructed. Star seemed to be calm, so Steffy moved on.

She snapped the lunge line onto Star's halter and began walking her in large circles. Steffy did as Parry had instructed, and Star began to walk in circles around her. When the little mare stopped and walked up to her owner, Steffy took a deep breath, positioned her lips accordingly, and blew her silky, red bangs away from her eyes. Then she started all over again. Over and over, she repeated the same techniques. The young equestrian knew that when the little pinto broke routine, she was only testing Steffy. The young trainer remained patient and consistent.

After her mare was walking circles around her, Steffy decided to tap the ground behind Star's hind hooves with the whip to get her to trot. Star responded with a trot, and Steffy was pleased by how well she was doing. Steffy worked her for a total of an hour and a half, and then she spent the rest of the time walking her pony around. It was beautiful. She walked her across the lush pasture and through the gorgeous woods. She enjoyed the crackling of the twigs and the small branches beneath their feet as they walked. Then she led Star along the crystal-clear creek running through all of it. She let Star drink from it after she was cooled off enough to do so.

After they finished their walk, Steffy tied Star up to the side of the barn. The young trainer in training groomed her little mare until all the dust was out of her coat. Then she carefully and gently picked up each hoof and tapped lightly on the bottom. She still couldn't pick Star's hooves, since they were overlapped, but she wanted her pony to get used to this procedure. So she went through the motions. The little mare was somewhat nervous about having her hooves handled. But her owner was quick and gentle, so she tolerated the procedure pretty well. Steffy was very proud of her, and she praised her and told her what a good job she was doing.

Then she heard the familiar sound of her mom's car as it pulled up. She put the brush box in the barn and grabbed the lunge line and whip. Then the girl kissed the mare's forelock. Then she ran to meet her mom. It had turned out to be a good first training session, and Steffy was excited to tell Sharon all about it.

Every day the little pony responded to her owner's training a little bit better than the day before. They were working very well together. The horse-crazed teenager was eager for Parry's next visit. She was eager to tell him all about the training sessions. His opinion meant everything to her, and she wanted to make him proud of her.

On one particular day, though, she went out to the barn, and an unexpected dilemma occurred. In the farmhouse next to the pasture lived another young teenager, who happened to be a boy. His passion happened to be shooting his BB gun at soda cans. Steffy had no idea what the neighbor was planning to do; therefore, she went about her business of training her pony as usual. Star was lunging nicely, so Steffy decided to extend her training session a little longer than the time before. She said to her pony, "This time, girl, we're going to trot a little longer." What happened next was an initiation into horse training Steffy would never forget.

As Star was lunging at a trot, the two seemed to be flowing together in perfect harmony. Then, like an unannounced missile, the boy next door began to fire his gun. The first shot caused Star to rear up. Then many more shots followed, causing the pony to run like the wind. Steffy remembered what Parry had told her about not letting Star get away with bad behavior, so she held onto the lunge line with all the strength she could muster. Star's eyes were so wide that Steffy could see the whites of them as Star looked back at her, terrified.

Then, as if her pony had no reservations regarding her crooked legs and overgrown hooves, that little mare took off at a full gallop, almost causing her owner whiplash. Steffy couldn't believe it. She was trying as hard as she could, pulling with all her might to get Star to stop. At this point, she would have settled for a slowdown. Star reacted to Steffy's pull on that line as if it had never happened. They both ran at a fairly good speed now. Steffy decided that, no matter what happened, she wouldn't let go. She was pulling hard, but Star was pulling harder. That little trainer yelled, "Whoa, girl! Whoa!"

Before she knew it, Star increased her speed, and Steffy ran faster than ever. She jumped over fallen tree branches and dodged huge rocks. Still determined not to let go, the feisty redhead kept running. She struggled not to get tangled up in the tall, thick brush Star ruthlessly pulled her through. Steffy still pulled on that lunge line with all her might. After they ran through the tall brush, the two found themselves weaving in and out of the standing trees.

Steffy felt her legs getting weak, and suddenly her knees gave out. She fell to the ground. Star now dragged her girl chest first across the pasture. She dragged her over the soft grass, across the hard rocks, in the dry dirt, and through the wet mud. Then, without warning, Star hopped over a ramp-shaped indent in the dried mud, apparently made by a tractor tire during a heavy rain. Steffy hit this indent hard, and it tossed her into the air a good couple of feet.

Her arms stretched out full length in front of her as her white-knuckled fists held on to the lunge line for dear life. Her legs stretched out full length behind her. For a few merciless seconds, that poor kid was in a straight line, completely off the ground. She resembled Superman flying through the air; only she was terrified, in pain, and covered in debris.

Her long, red hair blew straight back by the breeze, and she squinted as the mud and dirt from Star's hooves went flying toward her sweaty face full force. The next thing she knew, her pony ran through the ten-inch-deep creek. And that little mare landed her petrified girl smack-dab in the middle of that creek, with a stinging splash.

Steffy lay there for a few seconds, face down in the now-muddy water. The wind had been completely knocked out of her. Eventually she slowly pulled her face out of the creek and caught her breath. Finally, she managed to pry her eyes open one at a time.

Her long, red hair was matted and wet, sticking to her face. She was barely able to see through it. Then, when she was finally able to focus her eyes, she found Star at a complete stop, breathing hard and staring straight at her. Her pony had heard the splash, so she'd come to a complete stop to see what it was. She found her owner in the same position she had been in at midflight. She was belly down in a straight line and still holding onto that ever-loving lunge line. The exhausted girl realized the gunshots had stopped, and the neighbor boy stood next to the fence, looking at her. His jaw hung open, his arms dangling at his sides; one hand still held the gun that had started the entire mess.

"You hurt?" he called out to her.

Steffy slowly turned her face toward his voice and answered him with an attitude. Her voice cracked. "What do you think?" Then she began spitting pieces of dirt and grass out of her mouth. She managed to pull herself out of the creek and into a sitting position in the mud.

This little cowgirl was in a lot of pain pretty much everywhere on her body. She tried to remove her hair from her face with one hand as she held the lunge line with the other. She could feel the mud, sticks, and rocks that had flown into her hair. Steffy tried to pull as much out of her hair as she could, but it was no use. There was just too much in there.

Finally, she was able to get a better look at the boy next door; and when she did, she saw a very remorseful look on his face. The teenage cowgirl said in a semi-forgiving voice, "Well, my pride is hurt mostly!" Then she tried to give him as much of a smile as she could muster up. She added, "Do you think that while I am out here training my pony, you could *not* practice your shooting? It really scared her."

Then, wiping the mud off her face and looking as pathetic as ever, she said, "I will be out here every day for a few hours. Maybe you could practice when I am *not* here."

The boy, relieved that the stranger in the pasture next door was still alive, replied, "No problem. You sure you're okay?"

Steffy nodded and waved goodbye to him.

At first, she felt numb from her head to her waist, and she was pretty happy about that. Every place else on her body was prickling with pain. Then, when she finally started to feel her arms again, she was sure they had never felt so weak and stretched out. Her eyes still stung from all the debris that had been whipped into them.

Her thighs, feet, and toes ached; and as she pulled her torn-up blue jeans up past her knees, she found that her knees had been scratched up and were bleeding pretty well. She looked down at the front of her shirt, where a beautiful unicorn had once stood in a lavender background. Now it was caked with mud and grass stains. In addition, her beloved cowgirl boots were also covered in mud, and the tips of them were almost worn through from being dragged.

With the lunge line still in her right hand, and Star now grazing quietly at the other end of it, Steffy began to inspect her hands. The tops of them were reddened, all but the knuckles, which were still pale white. The palms of her hands were bleeding in areas. And where they weren't open and bloody, there were blisters already forming. Her hands stung and ached. With a lot of grunting and puffing, she managed to make it to her feet. Star munched on the tasty grass as she watched her owner. Steffy pulled on the lunge line little by little, bringing Star closer to her, grimacing in pain with each tug as she did so.

When Star walked up to her, the teenager looked her pony straight in the eyes and said, "Now that I know how fast you can run, I expect you to be cantering circles around me in no time. Come on, hot shot, we have more work to do before I leave." In spite of the aches and pains Star had caused, the determined horsewoman proved her words right. By the time her mom arrived at the barn, Steffy had Star walking, trotting, *and* cantering circles around her in both directions.

Sharon pulled up and got out of her car. She watched as her baby lunged her new mare. She smiled at Steffy as she walked closer to the gate. That was when she noticed her daughter's hair. It was still wet and matted with semi-dried mud. It still had weeds and debris sticking up out of it in places. Then she noticed her daughter's face was covered with so much dirt, she could barely see her freckles.

As Steffy lunged Star in another circle, her mom was able to get a better look at her shirt. That was when she noticed it was covered with mud and grass. Lastly, she spotted her wet, torn jeans; paying close attention to the torn-up knees. That was when her smile quickly faded into a frown.

"Steffy, honey, come here," her mom said with concern.

"Whoa, girl," Steffy said as she pulled on the lunge line and lowered her whip. Then, with a slight limp, she slowly led Star over to her mom. The baby cows had spotted Sharon when she first got there. They gathered up to the fence. She had no food to give them, so they settled for a pat between their ears. By the time Steffy and Star had reached her, the calves had left. Now that her mom was able to get a close-up view of her little girl, she couldn't believe what she saw.

"Oh my word! What in the world happened to you, honey? Are you okay? Are you in pain?" Her mom asked nervously.

Steffy kissed Star goodbye. Then she assured her mom that she was fine, just a little sore. Sharon assisted her daughter into the car and put the lunging equipment in the trunk.

On the way home, the aching cowgirl explained to her mom everything that had happened. She went on and on about her memorable training session with her pony. Her mom hung onto every word she said. She wasn't very happy about what had just happened. She began to understand that owning a pony was going to be a very big challenge for her daughter. When they got home, Steffy took a shower, and her mom tended to her wounds.

Then her mom gave her a couple of pain relievers and an ice pack for every place on her body that hurt. Steffy's dad smiled and shook his head when he saw her. He gently patted her on the shoulder and made sure she was okay. Then he told her he was proud of her and said to be more careful next time.

A week later, Parry came back out to the barn. He was very pleased to see that her pony was getting fit. He asked the teenager what she had been doing with her. Steffy told him she had been out every day, grooming and lunging her pony. She described the dragging session in detail. He couldn't believe she had held onto the lunge line.

In fact, he explained to her that it would have been better for her to let go of it once she realized she couldn't get Star to stop. Then, after Star calmed down and stopped, Steffy could have caught her, asked the boy to stop shooting his gun, and then resumed the training. The blacksmith chuckled to himself as he thought about a spin on words. Steffy's experience gave a whole new meaning to "training from the ground up."

Parry said with a half smile, "You know … there are two types of cowgirls in this world." Steffy waited through a short pause as Parry gathered some tools. Then he continued, "Those who have *been* hurt … and those who will *be* hurt." Steffy gave him a half smile back. She chalked her experience up as a lesson learned. Then she decided to move on from there.

The blacksmith began to get to work on Star's hooves. Steffy tied her pony up to the maple tree, and Parry began trimming. This time, however, Star stood there and let him do it. She moved a little from side to side throughout the event. But she seemed to understand that no one was going to intentionally harm her. Star was a pretty smart pony. She probably figured she could stand to be uncomfortable for a short time. She seemed to remember this hadn't lasted forever the last time. The blacksmith finished up relatively quickly. He was able to trim away some of the overlapping of the hoof as well but not much. He still had to take just a little bit of the hoof off at a time to prevent her from going lame.

Parry told Steffy he would like her to start soaking Star's feet in the creek after her workouts to reduce any swelling in her hooves. He also told her to get a bucket to take with her when she did this. That way she could gather up the cool water and pour it over Star's legs as well. He explained that she should pour the water, starting up as high as the pony's shoulder. She needed to treat her pony's legs *and* feet, since this kind of exercise would get them pretty sore.

But it needed to be done for Star to drop the weight. He finished by complimenting Steffy on doing a good job. After that she handed him ten dollars, and they said their goodbyes. She didn't know how proud of her he was. He didn't want to get her hopes up too high, though. After all, Star still might not pull through.

Every day for the rest of the summer, someone in her family dropped the horse-crazed teenager off at the barn, and then someone else picked her up later. Their little Steffer stayed there for about three hours total, really focusing on Star's training. She practiced voice commands with her pony like "Whoa," "Walk," "Trot," "Run," and "Back.' Star seemed to enjoy impressing her new owner, and she really liked the carrots and apples too.

Steffy would never forget how her pony had given her a run for her money. That little mare of hers was getting more and more healthy. And the better she felt, the more personality she had. Steffy thought she had better be ready for just about anything. She was very grateful for all the horsey experiences she had been given over the past few years. They had prepared her for such a time as this.

★ CHAPTER 9 ★

Star's New Home

ONE NIGHT WHILE Steffy was finishing up her chores at home, she overheard her dad talking on the phone. "Currant Road you say, between Day Road and State Road Twenty? Yes. I know the area. What is the cheapest you would be willing to charge?" There was a brief pause, and then her dad said, "Hmmm … I think she is a sheltie … No, no … that's not it. She's a little furry, fat pony … What's that, sir? Yes! That's it! She is a Shetland pony." He added, "So you'll take forty bucks a month? That seems reasonable. Okay, tomorrow at five o'clock? Yes sir, we will see you then."

"Steffer!" her dad yelled, thinking his daughter was in her bedroom. Steffy walked out from behind the living room doorway a whole lot sooner than he expected. She startled him so much that he grabbed his chest. His eyes widened, and he said loudly, "Oh my word! You scared me!"

His little girl covered her mouth with her hand and giggled. "Sorry 'bout that! I didn't mean to. What's up, Dad?"

He was still breathing a little hard when he answered, "I saw an ad in the paper about a horse for sale." Steffy sat on the couch next to him and listened carefully as he spoke. "So I decided to call the number and see if the owner boards horses as well. Turns out, he happens to have an extra stall sittin' empty, and he wouldn't mind a little extra money in his wallet. We need to find you a barn closer to home, Steffer. Don't plan on seeing your pony tomorrow. I need you to meet this man and check out his barn. I want you to make sure it is good enough for Star." Steffy nodded in agreement. She was pretty happy her dad valued her opinion.

The next day the two drove out to meet the man. His home wasn't too far from Al-Bar Ranch. Steffy's dad told her the man had two horses, his own and his neighbor's. As they approached the house, they noticed the man was standing in the driveway, waiting for them. He was a slender, somewhat older man, with salt-and-pepper hair, and he sported an overgrown mustache. But there was genuine sweetness in his eyes. As he watched their car approach, he smiled and waved. Mr. Hacker got out of the car and introduced himself to the stranger.

"Nice to meet ya. I'm Mr. Holme," the man replied.

Steffy's dad eyed the guy up and down. After that, he had a little small talk with the man to get a feel for his personality. Then when he felt comfortable, he motioned for Steffy to come out of the car. Then he introduced them to each other. Her dad was very protective of his girls, and whatever he said to this Mr. Holme, Steffy never did find out. He knew that if they chose to board Star at this barn, Steffy would be spending a lot of time there. As God would have it, the man turned out to be very nice and equally as kind.

Mr. Holme said, "Well, let me show ya the barn." The soft-spoken man had a slight southern accent, which Steffy took a liking to right away. She and her dad followed him back behind his house to the barn. "Now," he continued, "it ain't much, but it's mine. And I like to keep it clean, and I like to keep it safe."

The three of them reached the gate, and as he grabbed a hold of the gate latch, he said, "This here latch has ta stay secure at all times. Can't have none of the horses gettin' loose on me now." Steffy smiled and nodded in agreement; her dad did the same. As they passed through the gate, Steffy noticed a handwritten sign made from a piece of wood with white writing painted on it. It read, "No TreSPasSion." She smiled to herself and giggled a little under her breath. She didn't want Mr. Holme to hear her as she read the misspelled no-trespassing sign.

Mr. Holme pointed to a closed-in paddock. "This here area is for trainin' and such."

They all continued through to the other side of the barn. Steffy noticed that the outside of it was patched together with pieces of aluminum. Clearly the man didn't spend too much of his money on appearances. However, as they entered the inside of the barn, a sense of peace fell over the new pony owner.

The barn was very clean; even the dirt floor had been swept. All the grain containers had been neatly placed up against the wall, and they all had lids. The sweet-smelling hay was neatly stacked up at the end of the barn on skids to keep it up off the ground. Steffy knew hay had to be kept off the ground to keep it away from moisture. That way it wouldn't get moldy. Moldy hay causes colic, and colic can easily kill horses and ponies.

In addition, each of the three stalls had been mucked clean. The two stalls in use were filled with clean straw bedding, and the water buckets were filled with fresh, clean water. A clean grain bin with grain in it and three flakes of hay awaited each horse. Steffy opened and closed each stall door. All three doors seemed sturdy and strong. She was able to latch and unlatch them without any difficulty. She wanted to check them all in case, for any reason, her pony needed to be in any one of them at some point. Mr. Holme watched Steffy very curiously, and then he and her dad began discussing business.

The young cowgirl followed them outside. The sun was warm and inviting on her face. She listened as Mr. Holme pointed to a large field, saying, "Out there is where the horses will spend most of their time. I got a Tennessee Walker of my own. She's the brown one right there. She's the one for sale." Steffy smiled as she looked at her. Then her eyes caught a glimpse of a beautiful golden palomino mare. She had a white blaze down her face and a wild look in her eye.

"Who is that?" Steffy said as she pointed to the shimmering, golden mare.

"She belongs to my neighbor. They keep her over here so the two don't get lonely."

Then he quickly added as he looked seriously into the young girl's eyes, "You better keep your distance 'round that mare. She ain't too friendly! She was a champion barrel racer back in her day," he said as Steffy's eyes lit up. "But any more she's so dang mean and ornery that no one can ride her."

Boy, would I ever like to ride that mare! the young girl thought in secret. That little horsewoman didn't scare too easily. When her fiery sense of adventure shone through, the more a person cautioned her not to do something, the more she wanted to prove to herself she could do it.

She caught herself daydreaming about this palomino for a few minutes. Then she focused back on her dad and Mr. Holme.

She watched the two men shake hands again. Then her dad said, "Forty dollars a month? Hay and feed included, right?"

"Yep!" Mr. Holme said with a smile. "Just call before you bring out your mare, and I will have the other horses put up in their stalls. That way they can get acquainted with her slowly."

Tim answered, "Will do, partner." He returned the smile. Steffy also smiled and said goodbye. She liked Mr. Holme and his accent. And she adored his homemade, misspelled no-trespassing sign. She liked the way the barn was sturdy, safe, and clean. She could tell this man took good care of the animals on his property. His knowledge of horses was quite apparent as well. Closing her eyes with a smile, she thanked God for Star's new home.

The drive was about twenty minutes closer to her house, which would be a nice change for everybody involved. Steffy and her dad had nothing but good things to say about Mr. Holme during the entire drive. As soon as they got home, Tim made three phone calls. The first was to a coworker, Roy Heater, whom everyone had nicknamed "Cowboy" since he lived on a horse farm. The two men had met at work years before, and they'd worked a lot of overtime together. They'd struck up a friendship and discovered they had a lot in common. For instance, both men were fathers of red-haired, horse-crazed teenage girls. They were both very hard workers, and they both loved animals every bit as much as their daughters did.

Cowboy's daughter, Debbie, was a couple of years older than Steffy. Tim had taken Steffy to meet her at one of her Horse and Pony Club meetings sometime back. Steffy really admired Debbie and she had felt an instant connection with her the first time they met. Debbie had helped Steffy join the county Veterinary Science Club she belonged to. The two girls had quite a lot in common, and they enjoyed their friendship to the fullest.

"Hey, partner!" Steffy heard her dad say over the phone. He and Cowboy talked for a few minutes. Then he asked, "Do you think you could haul Star to a new location for us?" The two dads spoke a little while longer. Then she heard her father say, "The day after tomorrow?

That sounds good. See you Thursday then. You can follow us from my house. Thanks again. Over and out, good buddy," he added. Then he smiled at his daughter and gave her a thumbs-up.

After that, he called Mr. Holme. The two men spoke for a moment. Then he asked whether Thursday would be all right to bring Star over. "Thank you, sir," she heard her dad say. Then he hung the phone up and gave her another thumbs-up. Steffy was getting excited about the new barn. She was all smiles just thinking about it.

The third call he made was to Missy. "Hey, kid!" he said. "We are all set to take Star to her new home. We will need to pick her up Thursday evening if that works for you. Thank you for everything! What's that? Well, you are *very* welcome. Steffy is just thrilled with that pony. Okay, see you then. Take care now." Her dad gave his daughter a third thumbs-up. Then he let out a sigh of relief as he put the phone back on the hook. "Looks like we will be moving that pony of yours on Thursday," he said. The two smiled at each other, completely relieved that everything was working out.

Then, two of their three dogs and their cat came walking into the living room, demanding attention from them. They laughed as they gave the animals the love they were seeking.

The next couple of days seemed to go by quickly. Steffy hardly had any time to absorb it all. She was really nervous for Star to be moving to a strange place. It was very important for her to be able to see her pony every single day. She wanted to be sure her mare would know she wasn't going to abandon her. The concerned teenager found herself praying for Star to adjust well to her new home. She prayed wholeheartedly, "Dear Lord, would You please speak to Star's heart and her mind, and get her ready for this big change? Please tell her she will be fine. Give her peace and let her know she can trust me, no matter where I take her. Thanks, Lord. In Jesus' name, I pray, amen."

This Christian cowgirl believed that animals are very important to God. He tells us in His word that we must take good care of them, so she was confident He would answer her prayers. Steffy wasn't sad or worried anymore. She felt a lot of peace about the situation.

In the excitement of it all, she finally remembered to call Parry. She told him all about the new barn—about how clean it was and how good she felt about it. There was a bit of silence for a moment as Parry thought about the pony and her well-being. Then he said, "Steffy, now let's think a little bit about Star physically. Let's focus on her legs and hooves, and how this move may affect her. I don't want to scare you. But if the ride in the horse trailer isn't as easy and as smooth as the driver can make it, you might just have one very sore little mare on your hands."

He continued, "Remember, we are still at the beginning stages of Star's recovery, and we are not sure whether she will even survive. Don't get me wrong. You are doing a great job with her. I just need you to remember that she is still very fragile. Every time I trim her hooves, she has severe pain. Her hooves are so distorted, and the bones in her legs are so crooked because of them. I am afraid that any kind of transfer, especially long distances, could really set her back."

Parry cleared his throat and said, "Now, the first thing you need to do right before the transfer even takes place is to stand Star in the creek for twenty minutes. This will cool her hooves down and decrease any swelling she may already have." The young horsewoman listened carefully as he spoke to her.

Parry continued, "Also make sure you have your small bucket so you can use it to gather water and pour it on Star's legs too. And be sure to tell your dad you must do all of this so he doesn't expect to leave Star's old home right away." Parry was very concerned for this little pony, and he went on to say, "What I am hoping for is that the coolness from the water lasts until you get to the new barn. This will help Star more than you can imagine." He added, "Also, ask your parents to get some cool liniment. It looks like a bottle of rubbing alcohol, only it is a green liquid. It should be next to the rubbing alcohol at the store in the pharmacy section. Rub this all over Star's legs, from the top of her shoulders down to her hooves. If for some reason you can't soak her hooves in water, just use the liniment on her legs, and use it all."

Steffy just stood there on the other end of the phone line, not knowing what to say. She'd never thought about how this drive could affect Star physically. All she could do was stand there and listen to Parry.

"Now, this sounds like a done deal," he said, "so we need to take every precaution we can to ensure that Star has the best experience possible on Thursday. You will also need to make certain that you wrap her legs from the pastern to just under the knee really well to protect them. Star will need a blanket on her to protect her little body as well. And she needs to have lots of hay to munch on during the ride. This will calm her nerves and keep her mind off her hooves and legs." He finished, and the two said goodbye.

After they hung up, Steffy told her parents what Parry had told her. Then Tim called Cowboy. He let him know they would have to wait on Star for about twenty minutes before heading out on the night of the transfer. Then after that he called Missy and told her the same thing. Steffy's mom got right on her sewing machine. She asked Steffy's opinion about the measurements. Then the two of them made a simple, light-weight blanket out of an old bedspread for Star that night.

Before the teenage cowgirl fell asleep, she lay there in her bed, with one of her dogs curled up beside her. The other dog was in her arms, and her cat was sound asleep at her feet. She thought about everything Parry had told her.

She thanked God again for him. He was essential for Star's survival. Steffy knew she hadn't found this miracle-working blacksmith/trainer by chance. God Himself had planned it all in advance. With these thoughts in mind, she drifted off into a sound sleep.

Thursday came quickly, and Steffy gathered her first pictures of Star to show Cowboy and Debbie. They hadn't seen her pony yet, but Steffy had filled them in on every last detail of how they had found each other. She also gathered the leg wraps her dad had bought her from Al-Bar Ranch on his way home from work. Then she grabbed the travel blanket she and her mom had made. After that she took a handful of carrots from the fridge. She shoved the yummy veggies into the front pocket of her hooded sweatshirt. She also made sure she had Star's halter, lead rope, and liniment. Then she put everything but the carrots into a backpack.

It was now five o'clock, so the excited teenager ran outside with her bag to wait for Cowboy and Debbie. They were just pulling up as she reached the back gate. Steffy was smiling and waving to them as her dad came out of the house. Debbie jumped out of her dad's truck and jogged over to her friend. They gave each other a hug. Cowboy got out of his vehicle, and he and Tim shook hands. The two dads had one common goal in life: to make sure their little cowgirl's dreams came true; and according to both girls, their dads were pretty good at it.

Steffy pulled the pictures of Star out of her back pocket and proudly showed them to Debbie and her dad. Their smiles simultaneously turned into looks of concern as they viewed the pictures of Star for the first time. Apparently, they were both uneasy about what they were looking at.

"This is your pony?" Debbie asked.

"Yep!" Steffy answered. "And this is what her hooves *used* to look like *before* I found my amazing blacksmith." She pointed to Star's hooves.

Debbie said, "So her hooves aren't this long now?"

Her friend shook her head. "Nope. They are looking a lot more normal."

Debbie looked at the pictures again and said softly, "Are you ever going to be able to ride her?"

Steffy answered without any regret, "The blacksmith says no. He told me her legs are too crooked from the condition her hooves were in. But it doesn't matter to me. I'm just happy to have her."

Debbie nodded politely and forced a smile, but in her heart, she felt sorry for Steffy. She knew how hard her friend had worked to finally get this pony. She had been hoping she would get a barrel racing champion like her own mare. Nonetheless, Debbie could see how happy Steffy was, so she was happy for her as well.

Time was wasting, so they all agreed to get going. The father-daughter duos decided Steffy would ride with Cowboy in his truck and Debbie would ride with Tim in his car. The four set off to Woodland, Indiana. It seemed to Steffy like they got there in no time. She had talked on and on about her pony and that she was so excited to have her.

Cowboy listened politely, all the while trying hard not to show his apprehension regarding Star's condition. At the same time, Debbie talked on and on about the situation with Tim. She expressed her concern for Steffy. Owning a pony with such an extreme medical condition was a pretty big deal. Debbie gave her opinion to her friend's dad. She told him what a huge responsibility this pony was going to be. Tim listened carefully. But even with all Debbie's anxiety over the situation, he wasn't that worried. He knew Steffy would give Star's care all she had. He believed in her. He knew what his daughter was capable of.

Cowboy followed Tim to Woodland and up to the pasture, where Star was kept. Then he parked his truck along the side of the road behind Tim's car. Missy stood there, holding onto a rope she had loosely tied around Star's neck. Her husband and children were there too. They all wanted to say goodbye to Star. Steffy put the pictures of Star on the dashboard of Cowboy's truck and grabbed the backpack off her lap. After that she quickly opened the truck door and excitedly hopped out of it.

She sensed Star's anxiety and quickly calmed herself down. It was true; a horse or pony will take on his or her owner's temperament. Steffy wanted to reduce Star's stress in this move, not intensify it, so she walked up to her mare slowly. Then she reached out her hand for Star to smell it. As Star was sniffing it, her girl said, "Hey, I got you something." Then she began rubbing Star's muzzle with one hand as she pulled a carrot out of her pocket with her other. Her pony munched and crunched the carrot until it disappeared, leaving only a mound of orange pony slobber on the ground beneath her chin.

When she had finished, Debbie walked over to her friend and put her arm around her. Steffy had no idea Debbie was upset and on the verge of tears over this pony. Steffy, on the other hand, was all smiles. She stood there, just as proud as she could be of her pony, Starlite Mist.

There they were, two friends standing side by side, emotionally within two extremes. One friend was fearful, sad, and concerned. The other friend was proud, happy, and optimistic. While the adults were talking, Steffy asked Debbie to go with her to soak Star's hooves in the creek. Her friend gladly accepted the offer.

As Star stood in the shallow water, Debbie looked at Steffy and cleared her throat. Then she swallowed hard and began, "Um, Stef ... this little mare ... she isn't in very good shape."

Steffy patted Star on her withers. Then she looked at her friend and said quietly, "I know she isn't, Debbie."

"I mean, she could die, Steffy. I have never seen a pony in this bad of shape before. I have read about it in books, but I never saw anything like this in person. It's bad."

Steffy grabbed the little bucket and used it to pour water onto her pony's legs. Then she looked at Debbie seriously and said, "That is why God brought me here, Debbie. He sent me here to give Star a second chance at life. I know there is a possibility she might not make it. But I have to try. Look at her. She needs me. I am willing to give it all I've got. If she doesn't make it ... well, at least I tried."

Then a spark of hope appeared in Debbie's blue eyes, and Steffy continued, "Just think how awesome it would be if she *did* make it. She could live again. I won't ever be able to ride her. I know that. But she will be alive, happy, and loved. I won't be able to show her or win ribbons. But if she lives, that will be better than any ol' ribbon!"

Debbie looked at her friend, and now she understood. Then she said to her, "Well then, I think this little mare got real lucky. I will help you in any way that I can."

Steffy looked at Debbie gratefully. "Thanks, Debbie. I really appreciate that."

The three of them walked back to where everyone else was waiting for them. Debbie helped Steffy cover Star's legs from shoulder to hoof with liniment. After that, she helped her wrap Star's legs from the pastern up to just below the knee. She also assisted with putting the blanket on the little pony.

Cowboy opened the trailer door. Everyone watched curiously as Steffy led Star to the entrance of it. To everyone's amazement, Star cautiously lifted each of her short, little legs up high. And as carefully as she could, the brave mare climbed into that trailer like she was a pro. Steffy walked into it as well, on the empty side, and Debbie followed. She patted her pony and praised her, giving her a kiss. Debbie showed Steffy where to tie Star's lead rope. There was sweet alfalfa hay waiting for the pony to nibble on during the trip. Star found it immediately. Without hesitation she began digging into it right away.

Tim was so impressed with how well Star took to the trailer that he wanted to reward her with something. He quickly walked up along the side of the trailer to the window. Then he called out, "Star! Here girl. I have something for you." The adorable, little pony stuck her tiny head out to greet him. She had to reach her nose up and out the window, but she could see him out of the corner of her little eye. Her nostrils were flaring. Somehow she knew he was going to give her a treat. He reached into the front pocket of his sleeveless flannel shirt and took out a breath mint. Then he stretched his arm up to the window, and Star found the sweet treat with her upper lip. She swept it out of his hand and into her mouth without skipping a beat.

"That pony is somethin' else, I'm telling ya!" Tim said. "A month ago that animal wouldn't let a person near her. Now she is doing things like this." He gave Steffy a thumbs-up and said, "That a girl, Steffer." His little girl smiled shyly as she jumped out of the trailer.

Debbie said, "That pony looks much better than in her pictures. She has a really nice personality too. She's not a bad little starter pony for ya, Stef. She reminds me of my little guy." Debbie still had her first pony. In fact, he was now retired to a huge box stall, five luscious acres of grass, and all the love he could handle. Debbie never did let him go. She was now giving him the best last years of his life. Steffy just smiled. She knew Star was a gem, and she knew Star was meant for her.

"Okay," Cowboy said, "we have to get moving if we want to get this little pony to her new home before the sun goes down." Steffy hugged Missy and thanked her again for Star. Tim shook Missy's hand and then her husband's. Cowboy tipped his hat to them all, and Debbie waved goodbye with a smile. Then the four of them were off to Mr. Holme's farm, with Starlite Mist in the trailer. During the entire drive there, Steffy was turned around, facing the trailer. She wished she could be back there with her little dumpling. She kept thinking, *What if her feet are hurting? What if every little bump we drive over causes her severe pain? What if she becomes lame?*

She looked over at Cowboy and asked, "Cowboy, do you think Star is all right?"

He gave a smile and said, "That little mare is just fine. Did you see how she took to that trailer?"

Steffy said, "Yes."

"Well, she was telling us that she wasn't afraid and that she could handle the trip. If she wasn't sure she could handle it, she would have been reluctant to get in. And if you hadn't noticed, I am driving extra slow and taking it very easy over the bumps and potholes."

Steffy could breathe a little easier now. She trusted his judgment. After all, his nickname wasn't Cowboy for nothing.

Before she knew it, they were pulling into Mr. Holme's driveway. The teenage cowgirl was so excited and relieved to be there. Mr. Holme came out to meet Star and to make sure everything was going smoothly. Debbie and Steffy went right to the back of the trailer. Debbie opened the trailer door, and Steffy retrieved her pony.

Star didn't seem too nervous about the ride. She slowly backed up to the edge of the trailer and turned her little head around to see where she was. Then she carefully watched herself as she stepped each of her hooves out of the trailer and onto the grass. Finally, when she was completely out, she reached her head down and grabbed a mouthful of grass with her teeth. After that she quickly pulled her head up to observe this new place. She seemed very interested in the new sights and all the unfamiliar smells.

Debbie took Star's blanket off her and told Steffy to leave the leg wraps on for now. Then she explained to her friend that she needed to walk Star along the fence line of the property a couple of times. She wanted Steffy to orient her pony to her new environment before the sun went down. The more seasoned cowgirl walked with them the first time around. Then she went back over to where their dads were standing. After that she explained to Tim exactly what she was having his daughter do.

Star caught the scent of the other two mares and let out a full-bellied whinny. Her eyes grew wide, and her nostrils flared as she heard the other horses call back to her. She began walking much faster and a little sideways. She tried to turn around to face the barn. She seemed to be trying to catch a glimpse of the strangers that shared this new home with her.

Steffy could see how nervous Star was becoming, so she began to speak to her in a calm and confident voice. She talked about this new, exciting place. She told her about how it would be closer to her own home. She explained to her how much she was going to enjoy it here. She also shared with Star how proud of her she was for going right into the horse trailer. The young equestrian went on and on, talking about whatever she could think of to take Star's mind off being nervous. It worked, and halfway around the pasture, her pony did calm down. She trusted her leader. After the third trip around the big pasture, Debbie motioned for Steffy to come over to where she was standing.

"Now walk her around each of these paddocks," she said. "She needs to be familiar with all the parts of her new surroundings." Steffy did as Debbie said.

The three men walked into the barn. Then the two girls and the pony joined them. The other two horses whinnied loudly in a low pitch as they entered. Star answered back with a cute, high-pitched pony whinny, which made everyone smile. Then her owner led her right into her stall. Star's stall was in the middle between the two horses, and the curious pony immediately went over to each side of it to smell the others. The Tennessee Walker was very interested in her new stablemate. The mild-mannered mare seemed to enjoy the cute, little newcomer. The golden palomino, on the other hand, seemed to be rather nervous. Her eyes were wide, and her nostrils flared as Star reached in between the wooden boards of her stall with her lips to greet her.

Mr. Holme had Star's stall cleaned out and filled with fresh straw, bedded rather thick. The little mare seemed to enjoy the feel of it beneath her hooves as she was getting acquainted with her neighbors. He also had her water bucket full of clean, fresh water. Then the gentle-spirited man showed Steffy where Star's grain was and told her how much to give her. She filled up the small coffee can with grain. Then she went into her pony's stall and poured it into her grain bin. Mr. Holme fed the other two mares and instructed Steffy to give Star two flakes of hay. Then he gave the others their hay. All three mares were enjoying themselves, as they chomped on their grain, slobbering and grunting ever so shamelessly.

Debbie waited for Star to finish her grain. Then she tugged on Steffy's sleeve and motioned for them both to go into Star's stall. Together they unwrapped the pony's little legs. After that, Steffy gave Star a big hug. Then she kissed the star-shaped white patch of fur under her forelock. Debbie gave Star a scratch between the ears, and then the two girls walked out of the stall. Tim let himself into the stall and snuck Star another breath mint. Star took it from him eagerly and made a couple of pony chuckles, as if to say, *Thanks, Grandpa!*

Mr. Holme said he would leave all three mares in their stalls for the night to let them get acquainted. Then in the morning, he would put Star in a paddock alone so she and the other mares could take a little more time becoming familiar with each other. They would need to work out the pecking order among themselves. Everyone agreed that this sounded like a great plan. Then they all said their goodbyes.

Tim handed Cowboy some fuel money and gave him a handshake. "Thanks again, good buddy," he said with a smile.

The two girls gave each other a hug. "Thanks for everything, Debbie. I am so lucky to have a friend like you," Steffy said with a smile.

Debbie smiled back at her and said, "Me too." She warmly added, "Call me soon and let me know how Star is getting along here, okay?"

Steffy nodded. "I sure will!" Then she and her dad waved goodbye as their friends drove away.

After they said goodbye to Mr. Holme, they began their own journey home. Steffy was very happy with Star's relocation. She wrote in her diary that night about all that had happened. Then she sat on her knees and looked out her bedroom window. Gazing into the dark night sky, she prayed, "Dear heavenly Father, thank You so much for my pony. Thank You for her new home. Please be with her and help her feel comfortable in her stall. Please help her to fit in with her new stablemates." Steffy continued praying until she slipped from a kneeling position onto her bottom and then onto her side. Smiling, she snuggled her blanket up close to her chin. Her two smaller dogs and cat happily cuddled up next to her as she fell sound asleep.

The next day Steffy's mom bought another bottle of liniment on her way home from work. Then she took it and her daughter to the new barn. Before Steffy got out of the car, her mom looked at her and said, "Steffy, I am not familiar with everything you are doing with Star. But I do know one thing." She paused and added, "Star is really lucky to have you." She handed the bottle of liniment to her daughter and gave her a hug.

This gift made Steffy happy, and she replied, "Thanks, Mom. I love you."

Sharon smiled. "I love you too, honey."

The teen got out of the car and rushed back behind the house to the barn. She smiled as she watched her pony in her new environment. Star was eating the soft green grass as her owner approached her. The other two horses were on the other side of the fence, doing the same. It appeared that her pony felt comfortable here and was adjusting well.

Steffy didn't do any ground work with Star that day for fear of her legs getting sore. Instead, she gave Star a full-body massage and rubbed the green liniment into her muscles extremely well. Star seemed to enjoy it. Steffy sang songs to her mare and then she groomed her. After that, she braided her mane and then she braided her tail. Star didn't seem to be affected by the move at all, which relieved Steffy tremendously. Star was one very lucky little pony, and Steffy was one very happy little girl.

The rest of the summer went by quickly. Before Steffy could mentally prepare herself, eighth grade was upon her. She was glad she had time before school started to recover from the "dragging session." The blisters on the palms of her hands and the scrapes on her knees were all healed up now, and the scars were a reminder of her initiation into the wonderful world of cowgirls. Training was a great big part of owning a pony. Steffy smiled as she thought about what Parry had told her: *There are two kinds of cowgirls in this world ... those who have been hurt ... and those who will be hurt!"*

The day after Labor Day, 1985, was Steffy's first day of eighth grade. She couldn't wait to tell her seventh-grade Biology teacher all about Star. She made sure she brought the pictures of her pony to school. The first chance she got, she showed them to her. When Mrs. B. saw the pictures, she was so happy for Steffy. She asked her all kinds of questions about Star. The teenager was thrilled to answer them all. The excited eighth-grader was consumed with thoughts of her little mare galloping around in her mind. She also couldn't wait to show her pictures to all her friends.

The new pony owner found herself daydreaming about Star throughout the day. By lunchtime, her friends decided they would leave her alone to be in her own little world. They couldn't even hold a conversation with her due to her drifting off into deep thoughts of her pony.

It was now the end of the school day. Steffy was getting off the bus, and the only thing she could think of was getting back to the barn. As soon as she got home, she walked all three of her dogs. Then she gave her cat some attention. After that, she fed them all. Finally, the young animal lover grabbed three apples out of the refrigerator. Then she waited outside on the picnic table. Her little poodle, Tiffie was in her arms, and her big guard dog, Buster was at her feet.

Eventually, Cindy arrived home from work. Her little sister ran up to the fence with a hopeful smile on her face. Her big sister got out of her car, saying, "How do I already know what you are going to say? Is it my turn to take you to the barn? What the heck. I'll take you either way. Just let me do a couple of things before we go." Cindy took the little poodle out of her sister's arms and held her close to her chest. Then she gave the little dog a kiss on the head as she walked.

Steffy threw both of her arms up into the air and loudly yelled, "Yes!" Then she followed her sister into the house.

"Can you remember how to get to this new barn?" Cindy asked.

Steffy nodded and said, "Yep. It's on the way to Al-Bar Ranch. Just get on McKinley Avenue, and I can tell you from there." Cindy went into her bedroom and then came out a few minutes later. After that, she went into the bathroom and rehydrated her contact lenses with some eye drops. Finally, she checked her hair and makeup. Steffy watched her sister, admiring her. She thought Cindy was so pretty. Cindy was a mirror image of their mom and that is the biggest compliment any of them could ever think of.

Not only was her sister beautiful, but she was also very organized. She always made sure all her responsibilities were taken care of accordingly. Everything was always in its place. She was never running around, aimlessly looking for anything, because she always put her things back where they were supposed to go. She was never concerned about much, because she always made sure all her tasks were completed. She would always strive to arrive at her destinations early. She was rarely, if ever, late. Steffy could always count on Cindy. She hoped to be more like her as she grew up.

Finally, Cindy said, "I'm ready. Let's go!"

With apples in her possession, Steffy followed Cindy out the back door. They climbed into Cindy's car, and before long, they were headed to the new barn. Nearly fifteen minutes into the drive, Cindy said, "Okay, there is the road to Al-Bar Ranch. Now where do we go from here?"

Steffy pointed straight ahead and said, "We go over the railroad tracks. Then it is the first road on the left. It is called Currant Road." Their mom was like a walking dictionary and thesaurus. She had explained to Steffy that spelled this way, a currant is a berry. All three sisters thought their mom was really cool, because she was so smart like that. Anytime any of her girls had a question regarding English, you can bet Sharon Hacker had the answer.

"Okay, this is Currant Road, we are turning left, now what?" Cindy asked.

Her little sister eagerly looked down the road for familiar landmarks. "It's just up here a little ways. Yeah, it's right there. That brick house on the left," Steffy said, pointing at Mr. Holme's ranch home. As they pulled into the driveway, she said, "Thank you so much for the ride!" Then she hugged her sister goodbye.

"Someone will be here later," Cindy said. "What time do you want to be picked up?"

"How about eight thirty? That should give me enough time with Star."

Cindy smiled, and then said, "Okay, one of us will come get you. Love ya!"

Steffy called back, "Love you too!" Then she grabbed the apples from her pocket as she ran behind Mr. Holme's house to the pasture.

Star was by herself in one of the paddocks, grazing. The other equines were close by, on the other side of the fence. Steffy whistled to Star, and the little pony's ears perked up. She raised her fuzzy head up from the sweet, grassy pasture. Her owner stood at the fence and held out an apple. The little Shetland pony let out a cute whinny and quickly walked over to her. Star anxiously grabbed the apple out of her girl's hand. Then she quickly began to devour it.

Steffy let herself into the pasture. After that, she fastened the gate behind her. Quickly, she ran over to the fence near the other two mares. Steffy fed them their apples before Star had finished her own. This cowgirl knew how much Star would have enjoyed all three of the juicy fruits, but she wanted the other mares to feel loved too. She thought they might not be as hard on Star if she gave them attention also. Star was now the "new mare in town." Steffy wanted to help her fit in here, as much as possible.

Steffy patted her pony's cute little face and said, "Here, girl!" After that she made a kissing sound. Then she took her hands and patted the tops of her thighs. Next, Steffy began walking backward toward the barn entrance, and her pony followed her. "That's it, girl, come on!" she told her. Star followed her into the barn obediently. Then she stopped when her girl stopped. From that moment on, Star followed her owner everywhere. She knew Steffy loved her, and that made the little pony want to be with her.

The freckle-faced cowgirl grabbed Star's lead rope. She connected it to her pony's halter. Then she tied the rope to a hook next to the stall door. After that, she gave her mare a handful of hay to munch on. While Star was crunching away at her food, Steffy wrapped her arms around her neck and gave her a big hug. The pony's fuzzy neck smelled so good to Steffy. Finally, she took a soft brush from the brush box and began to groom her. Steffy started with Star's adorable face. As she brushed her muzzle, her pony nibbled at the brush. Steffy chuckled and asked, "Star, is there anything you *won't* eat?" The little equine looked at her with the cutest expression, as if to say, *Not really!* That made her girl giggle.

Next, Steffy gently brushed her pony's cheeks. Then she pulled her pony's forelock away from the white star on her forehead. After that, she kissed that little white star and leaned her left cheek up against it. She gently rubbed the sides of Star's muzzle with her thumbs and closed her eyes. She couldn't help thinking she might be dreaming. Then she smiled as she embraced the fact that her own pony was literally in her arms, and she still could hardly believe this was real. As Steffy continued to groom her, she looked at Star's pudgy neck. Then her smile faded as she realized that, as cute as that neck was, a thick neck meant health problems to a pony. It was a sure sign of overeating and founder. And it was said that if a pony had a thick neck, she could easily founder again.

When Steffy brushed Star's back and bloated belly, she was as equally discouraged. She knew Star was unhealthy. She had to make sure she did everything possible to keep Star from gaining more unhealthy weight. Finally, as she brushed her pony's tiny, crooked legs, she made a promise to herself and to Star. She promised that she was going to do everything she could possibly do to save her pony's life. She was determined to keep Star alive and give her a good quality of life. Steffy decided right then and there that she would increase her mare's workout time. She was committed to working off the thickness in Star's neck and getting rid of her pony's hay belly.

The young cowgirl untied her pony from the wall and draped the lead rope across Star's back. Next, she grabbed her lunge line and whip, and then she kissed at her pony. Star understood her. She followed her out of the barn and into a small paddock. This response gave Steffy confidence. She was even more convinced her pony was going to come out of this deadly condition she was in. Star followed Steffy along the fence line. When Steffy jogged, Star jogged. When Steffy walked, Star walked. And when Steffy stopped, Star stopped. This little mare was picking up on her owner's commands like she was born to do them. And Steffy was completely convinced her little dumpling was.

After leading her cute mare a few times around the paddock, the young cowgirl allowed her to smell the lunge line and whip. Then she gently touched Star with the objects all over her body. She wanted to let her become familiar with them in this new environment. When Star became completely at ease, Steffy hooked the lunge line up to her halter. Then she took the lead rope off and stepped back away from her. Finally, she began lunging her at a walk clockwise.

Approximately ten minutes later, she called out, "Whoa, girl!" Star obediently came to a stop. Then Steffy lunged her at a trot and finally at a canter. Then she brought her back to a trot and then down to a walk again. She then repeated all these steps while going in the opposite direction. At the end of the workout, both were sweating and tired. The young girl decided to cool her pony down by walking her along the fence line. After that, she took her mare out to the big pasture and finished cooling her off there. Star followed Steffy around like a puppy as the other two horses watched curiously. Every once in a while, the chubby, little pony reached down and took a bite of grass. They finally reached the end of the pasture. Then they turned around and began walking back to the barn.

The teen cowgirl had to hold onto the lead rope at this point, for Star was way too anxious to get back to where the food was located. Steffy knew she needed to teach her mare patience and that going back to the barn required control. She remembered reading a chapter about "barn sour" horses in a book. If a horse or pony is allowed to bolt back to the barn, he or she will try to do it every time, even while the owner is riding him or her. So this can become a very dangerous and even life-threatening habit.

Even though this young equestrian was told she would never be able to ride her precious mare, she figured she would treat her pony as though she had no handicap at all. She was sure this would help her grow to be the best little pony she could possibly be. Steffy didn't want Star to think she was different from other horses or ponies for a couple of reasons. First, she wanted her pony to be well behaved and safe. Second, she wanted her to have confidence and be happy too.

When they reached the barn, Steffy gave Star a full body massage. In her readings, she learned an owner's touch was one of the most important things a horse or pony could receive. The bond it creates is the foundation of trust.

It was pretty clear, from the way Star had been following her girl around, that the trust she had for her was growing stronger. Steffy wanted to make sure this continued. The ambitious cowgirl started with Star's muzzle and moved forward, massaging her face and then going down her neck. Star closed her eyes and seemed to melt with her owner's touch. Steffy could sense her relaxing as she continued massaging her back, then her belly, and then finally her little legs.

Steffy focused on the most crooked parts of Star's legs. She could literally feel where the leg bones had grown into a mangled state. The tendons had shrunk and grown very tight. She massaged each leg from the shoulder to the hoof for approximately fifteen minutes each. She worked the green liniment into the muscles. This seemed to be just what her pony needed. Steffy knew this would be a big part of their daily routine.

After the massage, she grabbed a pitchfork and wheelbarrow. Next, the ambitious teen began mucking out her little mare's stall. When the wheelbarrow was full, the teenage cowgirl wheeled it out to the end of the pasture. Then she spread the manure and dirty straw out onto the ground just as Mr. Holme had taught her to do. He said that when it is spread out in a thin layer across the field, the sun dries it up, and it decomposes back into the soil more easily.

As she headed back to the barn, the young cowgirl smiled. She was excited about the fact that she had just mucked her *very own* pony's stall. Just thinking about it made the butterflies in her tummy flutter. Then she put the wheelbarrow away and filled her mare's stall with fresh, clean straw. After that, she put a small coffee can full of grain into Star's grain box, and Star whinnied with excitement.

Finally, the young teenager untied her pony and led her into the clean stall. While Star was munching on her grain, Steffy grabbed two flakes of hay and tossed them under her grain bin. The adorable pony continued to devour her sweet feed. Her fuzzy, little head moved in circles as her tiny lips spread the grain all around the feed box. Steffy laughed at the sight of it. She thought Star just had to be the cutest, little pony alive.

As her little mare enjoyed her dinner, Steffy decided to clean out and fill her water bucket. She grabbed the hose and looked all around the barn for a bucket brush, but she couldn't find one. Then she thought for a moment. She needed to clean the bucket before filling it back up, but how? The only thing she could think of was to grab a handful of clean straw and use it to scrub the bucket. So she did just that, and—wah lah!—the bucket was yuck free. She rinsed it out with the hose, and then she hung it back up in Star's stall. Then she refilled it.

After that she gave her pony one last hug and kiss. While she was saying goodbye to Star, Mr. Holme brought the other two mares in for the night. Then he also fed them. "I'll do this for a few more nights," he told Steffy. "But then, unless it's stormin' or bad weather out, I'll keep the horses outside. They seem to like that a lot better than bein' cooped up in a stall."

The teen nodded in agreement, and then she heard the distinct, high-pitched *beep-beep* of her mom's car horn. Steffy said goodbye to him. She peeked into Star's stall and said, "Bye, girl. I will be back tomorrow. Be good! I love you!"

Finally, she ran out of the barn and around to the back. Then she let herself out of the gate, which she securely latched. Finally, she ran around the brick house to her mom's car. Both of her parents were there to pick her up that night. She gave them each a hug. Her mom asked, "So, how is your pony today?"

Steffy quickly answered, "Oh, she is just fine! She is cute and sweet and perfect." Then she buckled her seatbelt. Her dad was driving, and he put the car in reverse, and then pulled out of the driveway. At last, the three of them headed down the country road together. The happy thirteen-year-old was convinced she had to be the luckiest girl in the whole wide world. And she was sure the smile on her face was completely permanent.

Steffy repeated this routine with Star all week. She spent four hours every day after school with her pony. That first week of school went by quickly. On Friday, when her mom came to pick her up from the barn, she said with a smile, "Cheryl called. She wanted to know if she could spend the night tonight."

Steffy smiled big and asked, "Can she? Then she can come out to the barn with me tomorrow to see Star!"

Her mom smiled back and said, "Sure thing!" And then she drove straight to Cheryl's house. Steffy was smiling so hard that her cheeks hurt. When they got there, she let herself out of the car. In no time flat, she was up on Cheryl's front porch knocking on her door.

Her BFF answered the door with her backpack in hand and said, "I'm all ready!" Steffy chuckled to herself, thinking about how different they were from each other. Unlike her, Cheryl was always prepared. Her room was usually organized. One of her mottos was "A place for everything and everything in its place." Steffy often wondered how the two of them ever became best friends, since they were so different this way.

Steffy rarely made her bed. Her bedroom was completely

disorganized and messy (except for her horse figurines on her shelves). She was always searching for missing things, which in turn made her late for everything. In fact, with the exception of her dad, that girl spent more time looking for misplaced items than anyone else she knew. But for some reason, even with these differences, Steffy and Cheryl were inseparable, and that was that. God had placed them in each other's lives, and they were very happy about the arrangement.

That Friday night the two best friends stayed up way too late, singing and dancing to a unique mixture of Bon Jovi and Amy Grant. Before they fell asleep, Steffy looked at the calendar. It reminded her that there would be one more week before Star got her hooves trimmed again. She made herself a note to call Parry. She needed to give him directions to Star's new home. The two girls talked until they both fell asleep. Cheryl had Steffy's cat lying next to her, and Steffy had the beagle mix at her feet and her little poodle snuggled up lovingly in her arms.

Morning came, and the two girls made themselves a bowl of cold cereal. Steffy fed her pets, and the two best friends took the dogs for a walk. Then they gave the cat and rodents attention. After that, the ambitious teens waited for someone to take them to the barn. It was Steffy's dad's turn, and before long the three of them were on their way. Cheryl was really excited to go with to Star's new home. When they got there, she laughed under her breath at the misspelled no-trespassing sign. Then she eagerly followed her best friend into the spacious pasture.

Steffy gave a whistle and called to Star. Her little pony popped her head straight up and immediately spotted her girl. Then she walked as fast as she could to Steffy. She stopped quickly when she got right up next to her. Cheryl immediately stepped out of the way. She hadn't seen Star move that fast before, and the change startled her. She smiled nonetheless. Steffy had brought apples for all the mares. She gave Star her treat first, of course. The little pony completely consumed the sweet, delicious fruit, chomping it to mushy bits rather quickly.

Her little, black muzzle was now covered with white, foamy slobber. The two girls laughed at the sight of the mannerless mare. Then they gave the other horses their apples. They weren't quite as messy as Star, because the apples fit into their large mouths rather easily. The two larger mares were able to make their apples disappear without a trace.

Steffy whistled to Star, and her pony instantly followed her into the barn. Cheryl was impressed. Steffy could see the look in her eyes, and she smiled to herself. It took a lot to impress her best friend. Cheryl was happy Steffy and Star were developing a bond. Whether Star was looking for another treat or simply wanted to please her girl, either way it was a step in the right direction.

Steffy let Cheryl groom Star while she mucked her pony's stall. Then she showed Cheryl how to massage the little pinto and rub the liniment into her muscles. After that she let her friend lead the pony out into the paddock. Cheryl was more than happy to do it, and the two girls talked about everything from what their homework was for that weekend to what new songs were playing on the radio. Then they talked a lot about Star's progress and what improvements Steffy thought they might have made.

Cheryl wanted to know what Steffy was doing regarding Star's training, and Cheryl wanted to do it too. So Steffy showed her some ground work that consisted of jogging Star in straight lines, stopping her, and turning her. Then she showed Cheryl how to jog Star in figure eights, stop her, and back her up in a straight line. Cheryl even helped Steffy make up new routines for Star. She was really creative like that. Little Ms. Hacker admired that about her best friend.

Steffy had spent the past five years learning how to develop a close connection to horses, and Cheryl was every bit as interested in doing the same thing. Soon Mr. Holme went out in the barn to feed the mares. Steffy explained how to lead Star into her stall. Then she told her best friend how much grain and hay to give her pony. Finally, she showed her how to fill the water bucket. Cheryl was eager to do everything. Steffy thought Cheryl was a natural, and she was as equally impressed with her.

Soon the two best friends heard the familiar sound of the old green van pulling up in the driveway. The girls said goodbye to Mr. Holme. Then they both hugged and kissed Star. After that, they said goodbye to the other two mares. They could be heard giggling and laughing all the way out of the barn. The two girls were grateful for their friendship and they enjoyed every bit of their time together.

★ CHAPTER 10 ★

⊱ *Steffy's New Wheels* ⊰

STEFFY'S DAD HAD a few things on his mind these days. First, he was a little concerned his daughter's grades might suffer now that she had a pony of her own. He wondered whether Steffy would even try to get good grades now that she had nothing to work for anymore. Second, he and the rest of their family were a little tired of driving their beloved Steffer to the barn every single day, although they would never let her know it.

One day while browsing through the newspapers' classified ads, her dad came across an ad for a moped. He knew the law stated that as long as the vehicle had pedals, children thirteen years and older were legally allowed to drive them. No driver's license or license plate required. The price for the moped was a whopping $375, but Tim figured that since he didn't have to pay a dime to purchase Star, he was actually still ahead. So he talked the matter over with his wife, and they came up with another game plan. As long as their daughter maintained good grades and remained on the honor roll, she could get a moped to drive herself to the barn every day. They decided to discuss the decision with her after supper that night.

"Hey, Steffer," her dad asked. "How is school going for ya?"

Steffy smiled at him. "School is going good. I like it."

"And your pony—how is she doing?" Tim asked.

"She's doing pretty good. She is really getting the hang of this training business," Steffy replied.

Her dad nodded and smiled. "Looks like she's gonna get that second chance you've been talking about," he said.

Steffy's smile grew bigger. She waited patiently for her dad to make his point. He was still smiling, so she knew he must have something good to say.

"Well, Steffer, your mom and I have been thinking, and we have decided you need another form of transportation to and from the barn." Steffy couldn't imagine what he was getting at, so she listened to him very carefully. "Your mom and I both work long hours, and both of your sisters have jobs too. It's not that we mind taking you to see your pony; it is just that we would like to take it easy after a hard day's work."

Then he handed her the classified ads. "Look here," he said as he pointed to the moped ad.

"Moped like new, asking three hundred seventy-five dollars. Call after five p.m.," Steffy read aloud. Her eyes widened as she looked at both of her parents.

Her dad said, "We will get you that moped on one condition. You must keep getting good grades and stay on the honor roll. *Not again!* Steffy thought about how hard she would have to continue studying and earning good grades. But then she began to imagine having her own set of wheels. She continued to ponder the thought. *My own way to get to my pony? No more waiting on anyone? As long as there is good weather, that is. During spring, summer, and fall, I will be able to get to Star myself! I only need to depend on someone else in bad weather.*

"A moped of my own? That would be the coolest thing ever! Next to having my own pony, that is," Steffy said as she gave her parents a big grin.

The determined thirteen-and-a-half-year-old worked diligently in school that whole week. After lunch, instead of blowing off steam with her friends in the gym, she worked on her homework right there at the lunch table. She had to do her homework and study for her tests every chance she got. That way she would be able to take care of her pets at home, go out to the barn after school, *and* maintain a nearly perfect report card. She really wanted that moped. It would be wonderful to give her family a break and to have some independence, all at the same time.

One week went by, and Steffy was able to get A's on every homework assignment, quiz, and test she faced. After supper that Friday evening, she showed all her work to her parents.

"I called about the moped the same day I told you about it," her dad said. "I asked the owner to hold it for us until today. I figured you'd take me seriously about your grades. You proved me right. Good job, Steffer! Head out to the van. We are going to go look at the moped right now."

His daughter smiled at him, and then she jumped up and gave him a great big hug. Then she gave her mom one too.

"Just remember, you need to stay on the honor roll or you hand over the key." His daughter smiled and nodded in agreement.

Her mom stayed home while Steffy and her dad went to look at the moped. When they arrived at their destination, a blue, well-kept moped was in the driveway, waiting to be driven. A teen girl came jogging out of the house and up to the van, with her father following behind her at a walk. She introduced herself and motioned for Steffy to get out of the van. She got on the moped and asked Steffy to hop on the back with her. The two rode off together. All the while, the girl showed Steffy how to operate the machine.

Then it was Steffy's turn to take it for a spin. She wasn't nervous at all. Her cousin Jason had taught her how to ride mini-bikes and four-wheelers the summer before. So the adventurous teenager decided this test drive would be a piece of cake, and it was. She loved it.

She brought the moped to a stop and turned it off, giving her dad a thumbs-up. Before she knew it, Steffy was watching the girl's father collect money from her dad. She had to keep herself from screaming with excitement. That lucky, little redhead had just become the owner of her first moped. She was still in shock as the two fathers loaded it into the van. This was one amazing day that was for sure.

All the way home, her dad explained the very strict rules he and her mom had come up with for their baby girl. He told her the farthest away from home she could drive was to the barn. Then he told her she had to stay as close to the right side of the road as possible when she drove. Finally, he told her she had to use hand signals at all times. He explained that it wasn't her driving he and her mom were worried about. Rather, the other drivers on the road were the ones he didn't trust.

"Not everyone is a careful driver, Steffer, so you need to be extra cautious and aware of your surroundings at all times," her dad said. "Before we go home, I am going to show you the only place I want you to buy gas for your moped. Then I am going to drive you to and from the barn on the route I want you to take. You must take this route every time you visit Star."

Cell phones in households were still a thing of the future, and this dad needed to know where his daughter was going to be at *all* times. After all, thirteen was still very young, and with this kind of freedom, there came very serious responsibility. Her dad drove to the gas station on State Road 331 and Thirteenth Street, just two blocks from home, where two brothers owned and operated a modest, little filling station. He knew these men to be trustworthy individuals. He made it very clear to Steffy that she was to come only to this station when she needed gas for her moped. He wanted to keep a close eye on his daughter, so he figured that the stricter the rules were, the safer she would be. The two owners were glad to see their friend's green van pull up, and they both came out of the office with smiles.

The men said hello to them; then one began filling up the van. The three men chatted. Steffy smiled as they talked about her new moped and her pony. Her dad opened the van doors and showed the men Steffy's new wheels. The two brothers congratulated her on her hard work, and then she and her dad headed to the barn. Tim went on and on about driving safety, and he reminded Steffy that her curfew was still the same as it had always been. "Be home before the streetlights come on," he said. His daughter smiled at him.

Having three daughters can make a dad very protective. Steffy was thankful to have parents like hers. She considered them a blessing. The grateful teenager had two amazing parents and two great sisters. They lived in a nice house, and she had all the pets she'd ever wanted. Her dream had finally come true. She had a pony, and now she had a moped too. That night she thanked God for her family, her pony, *and* her moped. Steffy knew she was very blessed. She grabbed her diary and made sure to put in every detail of her amazing day.

★ CHAPTER 11 ★

Star's Rehab, Parry Style

TEFFY ALWAYS MADE sure her studies and chores were completed in a timely manner. Then she hopped on her moped and rode out to the barn every single, solitary day. Her dad made sure the route she took conveniently passed by Cheryl's house. Most of the time her best friend rode with her out to the barn and helped her with barn chores and Star's training. Steffy loved to praise Star. She made a big deal out of everything her pony did correctly. It seemed to be exactly the kind of encouragement Star needed to do her best. And she did do better every day.

The young equestrian called her blacksmith, and they made arrangements for him to come out to the new barn to trim Star's hooves back a little more. The day he came out, he looked Star over thoroughly. Steffy had bought a stethoscope from Jeffer's Vet Supply catalog through the mail, and Parry taught her how to take her pony's vital signs. She had also bought a soft tape measure Barry suggested to measure the circumference of Star's belly every few weeks. After they took Star's vital signs and measured her belly, Steffy wrote down their findings in her notebook to keep a record.

Parry did a thorough inspection of Star's legs and hooves. He had a look on his face Steffy couldn't quite define. He grabbed his tools from the back of his truck, and with Star tied to the fencepost he began to work. Parry stopped periodically, giving the little pony brief breaks. He was thinking rather intensely. Steffy could tell he was in deep thought. He was very quiet as he inspected and assessed each hoof.

Finally, he spoke. Steffy was very curious to hear what he had to say. First, he wiped the sweat from his forehead. Then he scratched his chin for a few seconds. After that he began gesturing with his hands as he spoke. Parry carefully explained that this little mare, just as he had suspected, had even more serious medical problems with her hooves than he'd first been able to identify. Parry was very careful as he chose his words. He didn't want to make Steffy anxious, but he knew he had to tell her what he was thinking.

He began with, "Steffy, I know how much you love this mare. And I told you right from the start that she was in really bad shape." He paused briefly, causing Steffy to become a little uneasy. "I even told you there was a chance that she might not make it, remember?"

Steffy nodded. Her nerves became a little more frayed.

The blacksmith continued, "Well, now that her hooves have been trimmed back, I am able to get to the heart of her problems. What I am going to do today with her hooves will cause her some pain. You won't be able to train with her for about five to seven days. Instead, you will need to begin very extensive rehab on her hooves." Steffy listened as he went on. "I am going to cut into the bottom of Star's hooves deeper than I ever have. It will hurt her. I expect to find more thrush, and if I am right, she will have many abscesses. More than likely, all four hooves will have them." Steffy petted Star as he spoke.

"The abscesses will look like little holes or slits in the bottom of her hooves. You won't be able to see it, but deep inside each one will be infection. Kind of like a really big, very deep pimple but worse and more painful." Parry went on to explain that at some point, Star must have overeaten and foundered. He told her about a bone inside the hoof called a coffin bone. When a horse or pony founders, the hoof swells with infection, causing the coffin bone to rotate. If it rotates more than 11 degrees, the equine goes completely lame. At that point the damage is done, and it is irreversible. It can get so bad that the leg bone could even collapse *through* the hoof.

He explained that after the hoof swells, the infection blows out the pastern; this is the bottom of the leg where the leg hair meets the top of the hoof. The hoof eventually shrinks back down to its normal size, except now it will have wrinkles in it, kind of like stretch marks. Then he pointed to the wrinkles Star had on her hooves. "We don't know how many times throughout her life she has foundered. And we don't know how long it has been since her last episode. So I suspect she could very well be in the process of foundering again. We are going to need to stop it before it gets any worse."

He continued, "She was lucky to have survived her first bout with founder. More than one run in with it might very well do her in." Steffy told him she had learned about thrush, founder, and abscesses in the books she had read—and also from her cousin Ami. Then she asked how exactly he wanted her to treat Star's hooves.

"Well, it will be a very long process, and you will have to be very diligent about it. If you aren't, she won't get better, and you will definitely lose her," Parry said.

Steffy looked at him with a serious expression. "I am willing to do whatever it takes. Just tell me what to do and exactly how to do it."

"First, I need to see exactly what we are dealing with here. Then I will let you know," he said. The concerned man grabbed a certain tool. After letting Star smell it, he picked up Star's right front hoof. He warned Steffy again that what he was about to do would hurt her pony, but it was necessary to expose the abscesses. The reluctant pony owner hesitated at first, but then realizing that it had to be done, she ultimately agreed.

As Parry began the procedure, Star moved from side to side. She held her little head up high. Her eyes were wide while she looked back, trying to get a glimpse of what he was doing to her. She was good, though. She put up with it, trusting both humans. Her owner was able to watch closely. There was some blood involved but not much. The blacksmith had cut out the first couple of layers from the bottom of each hoof. And just as Parry had suspected, he found several little slits all over the bottom of each one. He made sure Steffy saw them and was able to recognize the openings. He explained that after the bleeding stopped and the tender spots healed, Steffy would need to treat the rotting thrush and the infected abscesses. This was how she would have to do it:

First, she would need to put 10 percent bleach and 90 percent water into a spray bottle and shake it up. After that she needed to pick Star's hooves out. Then she needed to spray the bottom of each hoof with this solution. Treating her pony's hooves with this bleach mixture daily would kill off the thrush festering in Star's hooves, but Steffy would need to do something altogether different to get rid of those abscesses. She listened as Parry explained that the abscesses were very deep. The well-educated equestrian continued. He told her there was a very good chance the infection may have already reached the bones in Star's legs. If this was the case, Steffy would have to put Star down, no questions asked. He went on to say that only time would tell. Then he told her she should expect the worse, just in case.

Steffy was way too optimistic, though, but she never led on. Instead, she listened closely as he explained to her the next part of the rehab process. He told her she would have to start soaking Star's hooves in hot Epsom saltwater.

"This saltwater mixture will need to be boiling hot," he said. "As the hooves soak in it, the salt in the water will travel up the small openings in Star's hooves. Then, if we are lucky, the salt will break up all the infection and draw it out of the hoof. You will need to soak each hoof for fifteen to twenty minutes every day. If you don't, you are not going to get the full effect."

Then he continued, telling her she would have to do this treatment for the next several months, maybe longer, since Star's hooves were in bad shape. He stressed that the water couldn't be too high in the bucket. It had to be below the pastern. "Star won't be burned by the hot water, as long as only the hoof is immersed in it," Parry said to her. "Steffy, do you understand everything that I have told you?"

She nodded. "Let me grab my notebook and a pencil so I can write it down, though." Then she grabbed the items off the shelf in the barn and asked Parry questions. This young cowgirl made sure she didn't miss anything he was telling her.

Parry told her the abscesses needed to heal from the inside out. He explained that if they didn't stay open and heal properly, the infection would fester beneath the surface and eventually burst again. Steffy knew what that meant. Parry mentioned that he would like to trim Star's hooves one more time before a vet took a look at her. He wanted to be sure her condition wouldn't be reported as incurable and result in Steffy being forced to euthanize her mare. She assured him that she would start this rehab in the next few days. Then she would resume

Star's training in about a week, just as he had instructed. She paid him, and they said their goodbyes.

The young cowgirl was very concerned about her little dumpling. She lovingly held Star's face in her hands and pressed her cheek up against it. "Don't worry, girl. We are going to fix you right up. We can do this." That Christian cowgirl could think of only one thing at that moment, one of her favorite Bible verses. "I can do *all* things through Christ who strengthens me" (Philippians 4:13 NKJV emphasis added). She had no thoughts of ever giving up. There was way too much at stake.

Steffy got Star's stall ready with fresh, clean straw, a small coffee can of grain, and two flakes of hay. She filled up her pony's water bucket with cold, clean water and then told her goodbye. After that, she drove her moped home while thinking about Philippians 4:13 and believing it with all her heart. She had the faith of a child, and she didn't doubt God's word, not for one second.

When she got home, she explained to her parents about Star's rehab, Parry style. Her dad wasn't thrilled about having to buy new buckets to soak Star's feet, though. Then her mom came up with a plan. "I will cut gallon milk jugs in half, and you can use the bottoms of them as buckets. That wouldn't cost us a penny."

Her husband smiled at her. "Good thinking. And I know that the feed store will be able to get the Epsom salts in bulk for us, so that should save us some money too."

Sharon got busy emptying and cutting the recycled milk jugs she used to water her plants. Tim and Steffy made it to the feed store before it closed. Sure enough, the store had the Epsom salts they needed. The father-daughter team bought a few bags of it.

After they returned home, Tim called Mr. Holme and explained to him what Steffy had to do to rehabilitate Star. The precious man offered to boil water for her every night. However, he said there may be a few days here and there when she would have to bring the water from home. He had plans to go on vacation. He said he would call as those days approached to let them know when that would take place.

That night Steffy prayed, "Dear Jesus, thank You again for Star. I really love her. But Lord, she is in really bad shape. I need to do a lot to make her healthy again. I know I can't do any of this without You. Please guide me as I treat her hooves. Please send the saltwater up to each abscess as far as it needs to go to draw out all the infection. And please heal her thrush by making the bleach water work as hard as it can. Thank You. I love You. Amen."

Steffy rolled over onto her side and then drew her legs up a little to get comfortable. Her pets were in their usual positions on her bed as she drifted off to sleep. That night she dreamed she was riding Star through the pasture at a gallop. The day was warm and sunny, and Star was as healthy as can be. A warm breeze blew through her hair and also through Star's mane and tail. It all seemed so real. The happy teenager woke up with a smile in the morning, and she greeted each of her pets with a hug and a kiss. It was Sunday, and she completed all her chores. Then she walked each of her dogs before she and her sister Sandy left to go to church.

Just as on any other Sunday, the two of them stopped to pick up as many kids as they could find. When they got to church, Steffy was happy to update her friends on Star's progress. They were always excited to hear how her pony was doing. She also asked them to pray for Star. Her Sunday school teacher had the entire class pray together; this helped take away some of the anxiety Steffy was feeling. After they praised God and learned more about Him, church ended. Then Steffy and her sister returned all their friends back to their homes.

When she and Sandy arrived back at their house, Steffy placed all the items she needed for Star's therapy on the kitchen table. Then she began stuffing them in her backpack. First she placed inside, the bags of Epsom salts, a measuring cup, and a spoon. Next, she arranged the bottom halves of the four milk jugs inside the bag. After that she carefully wedged in a new notebook, some pencils, a large eraser, and a small pencil sharpener. When she was finished with all that, Steffy carefully managed to put her backpack on. It was quite bulky, but she figured she would be able to balance it on her back just fine as she drove herself to the barn.

Her dad had been watching her from the living room. He thought for a few minutes, and then he came up with an idea. Tim had his daughter go with him into the garage. He searched until he found a plastic milk crate and some bungee cords. Then he wiped the crate down. After some trial and error, he managed to secure it onto the back of his daughter's moped. "There. Now you don't have to wear your backpack. You can put it in the crate," her dad said proudly as he smiled at his little girl.

The grateful teenager gave her dad a hug. "That's awesome, Dad." Then she placed her backpack inside it. The bag stuck out of its container here and there, so the teenage redhead did some quick manipulation and stuffed it down as snug as she could. "It fits perfectly," she assured her dad. After that, she got on her moped and started it. She looked back at her new crate and looked at her dad. They simultaneously gave each other a smile and a thumbs-up. Finally, she was off to see Star.

Once she was at the barn, Steffy sat in the grassy paddock with Star at her side. Her pony was munching away on the tasty green grass while her owner awaited Mr. Holme's arrival. She needed a large bucket of boiling hot water so she could start Star's therapy. She had her notebook and a pencil in hand as she wrote down a new schedule. It looked something like this:

1. Give Star treats.
2. Soak each hoof fifteen to twenty minutes.
3. Spray hooves with bleach water.
4. Massage Star.
5. Apply liniment to legs and walk or jog her for one hour.
6. Lunge Star for ten minutes in each direction.
7. Cool Star off.
8. Clean stall and barn.
9. Feed and water Star.

That horse-crazed teenager may not have been very organized with anything else in her life, but her time with her pets, including Star, was scheduled down to the minute. Before long, Mr. Holme was home, and he brought out a bucket of boiling water. He had it covered with a lid to keep it hot. Steffy thanked him for his help, and the southern gentleman smiled at her. He was curious, so he decided to stick around and see what she was going to do next.

First, the determined teenager tied her pony up to the outside of her stall. Then she got the salt and the homemade "buckets" out of her backpack. He watched as she lined the milk jug halves in a row on the ground. Then she poured approximately half a cup of salt into each one. Next, she filled them almost half full of hot water. After that she stirred them up with the spoon. Then, she held the mixture up to her pony so Star could see and smell it. Then she spoke softly to her as she placed each "bucket" on the ground next to Star's legs. Finally, she put each hoof into its designated bucket. Unfortunately, Star kicked every one of her hooves out of them, dumping the water onto the barn floor. So Steffy had to start all over again.

Luckily, Mr. Holme had brought out plenty of water because Star wasn't cooperating very well. The ornery little mare kept dumping the water repeatedly. Finally, Steffy decided she would have to do this a different way. She thought about it and realized she was going to have to soak one hoof at a time, so that was what she did.

This appeared to be working, so Mr. Holme decided to leave the girl and her mare alone to get the rehab completed. He walked away with a smile, shaking his head. The man wondered why someone would want a pony in that bad of shape, but at the same time, he was proud to know someone who would care for an animal like that. Then he thought back to when he had been a boy and realized Star was good for Steffy. That little mare would keep the teenager busy and out of trouble, and that was a good thing.

The determined girl managed to hold her mare's crooked little leg as Star's hoof soaked for fifteen minutes. Star kept trying to pull it up out of the water, but Steffy wouldn't let that happen. The young girl thought it must have felt strange to her pony when the abscesses began to drain. Maybe it hurt or at least caused some kind of weird feeling, like an itching sensation or something. She wondered whether it may have been similar to when her mom gave her cold medicine for a stuffy nose and her sinuses drained. It just felt odd.

The teenage cowgirl ended up moving Star to a dry location in the barn so she could sit on the ground. Squatting was getting tiresome, so Steffy switched it up a little. Some of the time she sat on her knees. Some of the time she squatted, but most of the time Steffy was on her bottom, sitting cross-legged and holding each hoof one at a time in the hot saltwater. Star was a stubborn little mare, and she gave her owner a hard time with this part of the rehab. Steffy knew it would take her pony some time to get used to the procedure, so she was very patient with her. Finally, the determined girl was able to get the job done. She then washed the buckets with bleach, rinsed them out, and set each of them upside down on top of four fence posts to dry.

After that Steffy began to massage Star's entire body. When she got to her legs, she rubbed each down with liniment, from shoulder to pastern. The young girl applied more pressure to the most crooked areas of her pony's legs. Star became completely relaxed. Steffy watched as her pony's sleepy eyes grew heavy. They were half open for a short time, and then they finally closed altogether. The content pony had fallen asleep while standing there, getting a massage. Steffy thought it was the cutest thing she had ever seen. Star gave out a few grunts, and before long, she was snoring. Her bottom lip gave in to gravity, and it just hung there, exposing her teeth. The sight was so adorable Steffy could hardly stand it. She smiled as she watched her precious "sleeping beauty."

The young cowgirl couldn't help but bubble up inside with happiness. *God is so awesome,* Steffy thought. *He created this precious little pony, and I was the lucky one He chose to enjoy her.* She felt so blessed to have Star as her own, and she felt honored to be the one to rehabilitate her.

The determined pony owner continued this therapy for the next week, and it seemed that Star looked forward to it. The little pony soon allowed her girl to soak her hooves simultaneously, the way Steffy had originally tried to do it. The teenage cowgirl was very happy about that development. It saved her quite a bit of time. There Star stood in the barn, with all four hooves soaking in the bottoms of milk jugs. The sight was so cute and pitiful, all at the same time. *Well, at least her hooves aren't long enough to be poking up out of the water now,* Steffy thought.

After that first week had gone by, the teen equestrian was able to incorporate the rest of Star's routine back into her visits. The weather was exceptional for being autumn, and the two began exploring the countryside together. Steffy led Star down the country road, sometimes at a walk, other times at a jog. One day they discovered an old, abandoned house. It was very small. It had white siding on it and an old western fence encircling it. It was locked, so Steffy couldn't go in. But she pretended to live there on her "ranch," with her mare out back, grazing in the pasture, just like in the old westerns she and her dad would watch on television together.

When she finished daydreaming, they walked farther down the road, discovering different sites. The two found interesting bugs to look at. Steffy enjoyed making wishes as she blew the pollen off the aged dandelions. This was exactly where Steffy wanted to be. She loved the fact that she finally had Star. Her dream was now a reality, and she was thoroughly enjoying every bit of this part of her life. She jogged her pony for a little while longer, and then she walked her back to the barn. When they arrived, she cooled Star off, mucked her stall, and then finished everything on her schedule. She left her notebook there at the barn with a couple of pencils. Then she put her rehab supplies on the shelf near Star's belongings. After that the young girl said goodbye to her little pony and drove away on her moped.

She spent the rest of the day with her best friend, Cheryl, Darnelle, and many of their other friends. The teenager was sure to be home by the time the streetlights came on. She had a little time to get her homework organized before she went to bed that night. During those next two weeks, the teenage cowgirl settled into her routine quite comfortably. She was able to do everything Parry had instructed her to do. Steffy was happy with herself, and Star loved all the extra attention. Mr. Holme played a very big role in Star's rehab too—and he was right. Star was good for Steffy, but he had no idea just how good. Star was Steffy's biggest wish, a young cowgirl's dream come true. A Christian teenager's answered prayer. This cute little mare was extra special.

★ CHAPTER 12 ★

Star's Extensive Training

PARRY SHOWED UP bright and early on the next scheduled Saturday morning, and he was very pleased by the rehab Steffy had been doing. It was obvious she was soaking Star's hooves every day. The young equestrian was going above and beyond what Parry had asked her to do. She was giving Star a full-body massage and jogging her several miles a day down the road and back. It hadn't been that long since Steffy started the specialized care, and Parry was beginning to be more optimistic.

He didn't mention the possibility of needing to put Star down this time. Instead, he looked at Steffy and said, "Well, I have to say, she is definitely getting better and not worse. I like the fact that you are on top of your game here, young lady. I have to admit, I was really worried for this pony up until today. I still am to an extent. But you are proving to me that you are diligent about her care, and this gives me a lot of hope.

"There is still a chance that the abscesses may have gone too far, but the thrush in Star's hooves is almost gone. I am becoming more convinced that she is going to beat both the thrush and the founder. Only time will tell." The blacksmith petted Star's neck and scratched between her ears every so often as he spoke. "You are doing exceptionally well, but I am thinking we better start working on your pony's behavior. Once she is in better shape physically, she is going to start challenging you more to see what she can and cannot get away with.

"She is a pony, and she is as smart as a whip, so you will need her to behave. Otherwise, she can become dangerous, and that wouldn't be good," he continued. Parry asked Steffy to grab her notebook and pencil. The young girl quickly retrieved them. She would need a lot of items from home the next time he was out. She wrote as he spoke, and her list looked like this:

Star's Extensive Training Supplies

1. Two trash bags, one paper grocery sack
2. One pot, one pan, one big wooden spoon
3. One large metal coffee can with a lid, full of nuts, bolts, or screws
4. One umbrella
5. One roll of aluminum foil
6. Some big balloons, a pin
7. Anything else I can think of that is noisy, shiny, loud, or crunchy

Parry explained that now was the time Steffy needed to really get Star to trust her in any given situation. Since they were jogging on the road, Star needed to be safe—not just for her own sake but for Steffy's sake and for the sake of the public as well. Parry felt a sense of responsibility for this little girl, and now that he had agreed to help her rehabilitate her pony, he needed to be sure Star was safe for her. If anything happened to Steffy, he would feel responsible. He felt as though he had to do everything he could to keep this little horse lover safe. Parry knew Steffy was going to rehabilitate this little mare with or without his help. And he knew he could give her a really good start, so he promised himself he would give the young girl the necessary training to do it right, and that included pony manner training.

Steffy was at the barn every day after school and every weekend for the next three weeks. She told her family what Parry had told her, and they made sure their Steffer didn't miss one day. That fiery redhead was determined to complete her pony's rehab, regardless of the weather. On rainy days, her family made sure to take her to the barn so she wouldn't get drenched driving on her moped.

From all the hoof soaking to cure the abscesses to all the bleach water therapy to cure the thrush in her pony's little hooves, Steffy remained diligent about her pony's care. In all the jogging for miles up and down the country roads, the young equestrian worked hard to strengthen her little mare's crooked legs. By lunging her pony daily in the paddock to improve Star's weight, Steffy took great care in making sure she never missed a day of exercising her little dumpling. In addition, the driven teenager was diligent about giving her pony full-body massages daily, to soothe her mangled legs.

For three more weeks, she was Star's nurse, and she took her job very seriously. She rarely saw much of her friends, but they all knew why, and they understood. As far as the ambitious little redhead was concerned, her pony was either going to pull through this dreaded state, or *she* was going to pull through this dreaded state. Those were her only two options, period.

Parry called Steffy the morning he was to come out again, and he went over the list of all the items she was to bring with her to the barn. He made sure he asked Steffy whether she could get a ride to the barn, because she wouldn't be able to bring everything on her moped. Steffy assured him that she had everything ready to go and that she had a ride. They agreed on a time, and she was there, as planned, with all the items on her list.

The blacksmith/trainer arrived and instructed the young girl to lead her pony out to the big pasture. Then he put the other horses in their stalls. "Okay, is there anything Star doesn't allow you to do?" Parry asked.

"Yes, she hates for me to give her a bath. She tries to get away from me constantly. She moves all around, and I can hardly get her bathed. The last time I tried, it rained, and that was the only way she was able to get rinsed off. I don't know why, but she acts terrified of water."

"All right, I will keep that in mind. Now I am going to need her to lie down while we do this. It is the safest place for her to be. I am going to tie a rope around her right front leg, just above her hoof. Then I am going to gently and slowly pull it toward her rear legs. She will begin to kneel onto her knees, and then she should lie down on her side. It's no different from when she lays herself down on the ground to rest or scratch her back. You have seen her lie down and roll before, haven't you?"

"Yes, I have, and she is so cute when she rolls on the ground," Steffy answered.

He assured her that he would be very gentle. He said her pony would be comfortable and that she shouldn't worry about this procedure, because if she felt uncomfortable with it, her pony would too. So Steffy did as Parry said, and she trusted him as he laid Star on her side. In turn, Star trusted Steffy. The cute little pinto liked to lie down to rest and to roll, so this part of the training didn't seem to bother her at all.

Now the tough stuff was about to begin. Neither Steffy nor Star had a clue what they were in for. Ready or not, they were about to find out. Parry wasn't exaggerating. There was a lot involved in Star's extensive training. First, Parry had Steffy sit on the ground and lean on Star's neck as he began the process. He instructed her to speak calmly to her pony. He told her to pat Star's neck as she reassured her that everything would be okay. He explained every procedure before he actually did it so the teenager would know what to expect. Then he told her what kind of results he expected to get from each one.

Next Parry grabbed the garbage bag and allowed Star to smell it. Then he lightly rubbed her muzzle and face with the bag. After that he touched the bag along the pony's neck and back. Next he took it down her legs, belly, and buttocks. Lastly, he held the bag like he was wearing it like a glove, and then he ran it down her tail. He told Steffy that by introducing the items to Star in a nonthreatening way, she would become desensitized to them. This would make her much more trusting and, in turn, safer. As he made things noisy, she would get used to the objects and be less afraid of what they could potentially sound like. By touching her with them, she would learn not to fear new things, even if they were unfamiliar and noisy, and came close enough to touch her.

In the beginning, Star took in a deep breath while smelling the garbage bag. She was fine with it being rubbed on her body, but then Parry started getting very noisy with it. He shook the bag open, slowly at first, and then began to vigorously make noise. Then he made it touch Star's face and around her ears. He did this until she became comfortable with it. Parry began to make noise with the bag as he rubbed it down her legs and across her belly. Star squirmed to get away from it at first. But then she eventually realized it wasn't hurting her, and she grew used to it. He ran it down her tail, making it as loud as he could. He told her owner to remain calm and to speak quietly to her mare the entire time. Star tried to thrash her head around, but Steffy's weight wouldn't allow that to happen. Then she tried to kick and get up, but her legs were tied together, and she was unable to do so.

When Star finally calmed down, Parry gave her a break, petted her, and told her how well she was doing. Then he got another item and did the same thing all over again. The next thing on the list was the brown paper bag. He introduced it to Star, first by letting her smell it, then by rubbing it all over her body. He put it to his lips and blew it open with a deep breath of air. Then he smashed it. Then he opened it up the same way, and he smashed it again. He did all of this while he was touching her with it.

Again, Star tried to move her head and legs, but Steffy remained calm and was able to bring her pony into a more relaxed state as well. Every time Star finally accepted the scary noises, Parry stopped. Star was finally getting the idea; whatever she was faced with, no matter how scary it appeared, wouldn't hurt her. In addition, the minute she accepted the object, it stopped making terrifying noises, and it went away. This pony began to understand that just because something was unfamiliar, that didn't mean it needed to be feared. She was getting the idea that new things could be tolerated, even if they weren't understood.

Star trusted Steffy; that much she knew. So come what may, that little pony was determined to face the scary stuff with courage. Finally, Parry finished by blowing air into the bag one last time and popping it as loudly as he could. Star had become so comfortable with all the previous noise that the popping of the bag barely fazed her at all. The gentle man was very pleased with Star's reactions so far.

Parry continued to give Steffy and Star a few breaks in between the items on the list. And then he resumed the training. The seasoned trainer introduced the pot and pan to the little mare. Then he introduced her to the wooden spoon. After that, he used the wooden spoon to hit the pot and pan. First, he hit them softly and slowly, then loudly and quickly. After that he hit them to a certain beat. Sometimes he created a nice melody. Sometimes he hit them in an array of annoying noises. He kept this up until Star accepted all of them. Then he stopped and moved on to the next item on the list.

Parry grabbed the metal coffee can Steffy had brought. It was filled halfway with screws, nuts, and bolts. He introduced it to Star. First, he let her smell it, then he began shaking it lightly, and then he shook it vigorously. Star lay there, not even flinching. Steffy continued petting her face and neck. It was just the reaction Parry had been hoping for. He then took the umbrella and opened and closed it numerous times all around Star's face. It was noisy and strange, but the precious pony trusted her owner, and she lay there quietly. She seemed to enjoy the petting and all the attention Steffy was giving her as well.

Then Parry used the shiny, noisy aluminum foil and the blowing and popping of latex balloons in the training. Still Star just continued to lie there, not appearing to care about the noises at all.

"Well, all righty then," he said. "It looks like we have accomplished what we set out here to do today." He untied Star's legs and instructed Steffy to encourage her pony to her feet. The little mare got up slowly. Parry then told her owner to take her over to the water trough and offer her some water. Steffy did as she was told. Star put her cute, little muzzle in the water and moved her head all around, playing in it. Then she took a short drink and seemed satisfied with that.

The three of them were exhausted. They were all sweating and breathing hard. This training had been quite the workout. Steffy put her hands on her hips and blew her red bangs from her face. She smiled at Parry, and he smiled back. Then Star looked at her, then she looked at Parry, and then she yawned. After that the little pony shook her head back and forth. Then her neck and the rest of her body followed, shaking much of the dirt off herself.

Parry then told Steffy to tie Star up and bathe her. The exhausted girl looked at him as if to say, *You want me to do what?* Parry knew what she was thinking, and he smiled and said, "Go ahead. See what your pony does."

Okay, Steffy thought as she tied her up. *But I don't think she's gonna let me.* The young equestrian collected the hose anyway and turned the water on. She approached Star and allowed her to smell the running water. Star looked at the hose and running water, and then she looked away. She was covered in sweat, she was worn out, and she didn't even seem to care that the hose was near her.

"Go on, give your pony a bath," Parry instructed.

Steffy did as she was told, gently spraying Star. She started at her hooves and worked her way up each leg. Then she sprayed the rest of her body. Star stood there as if she were getting a body massage. She didn't move at all. Steffy couldn't believe this was her pony.

"Now give her a good hosing down every day, and she will accept it as part of her routine," Parry said confidently. "You won't be doing that in the winter months, of course, but come next spring, she should still be fine with baths. Now that she can trust you in noisy, scary situations, she will be much safer for you, especially on the roads with loud trucks and horns honking. You did a fine job with her training. She's a good little pony." He smiled.

Steffy finished Star's bath. Then Parry scratched Star's wet forehead. After that he gathered his tools and trimmed her hooves. Star just stood there, literally falling asleep as he worked. Steffy couldn't believe the difference in her pony. She was amazed by the progress they had made in just one afternoon.

The teenage cowgirl paid Parry. Then they scheduled for him to come out again in another three weeks. Before collecting the payment and leaving, he told her to incorporate the noisy items they had used in the training session into their everyday routine. This way Star would be constantly desensitized to the scary objects and noises. The exhausted teenager agreed to do so. Then she said goodbye to their amazing trainer, and put her little dumpling into her stall. After that she gave Star grain, hay, and fresh water. When she had finally finished all her barn chores, she plopped down on a few hay bales. Steffy yawned, stretched, and curled up into a comfy position. Then she closed her eyes. She needed to rest a little bit before someone in her family arrived at the barn to get her.

Star ate, and then she too lay down in her stall. Soon the two of them were fast asleep. They had both learned a lot that day. Steffy had learned to trust Parry, and Star had learned to trust Steffy on a much larger scale. The lessons they had learned were invaluable. There was no amount of money that could have paid for that kind of training, and Parry didn't even ask for anything in addition to his hoof-trimming fee. This experience reminded the teenager that there truly were good people in this world; and Parry the blacksmith was one of them.

Day after day, week after week, Star trusted Steffy more and more.

They became one unit. Steffy was Star's, and Star was Steffy's. Their bond was unlike anything either had ever experienced before. That little pony followed her owner everywhere. Steffy was able to bathe her effortlessly at any given time. And everything Steffy asked Star to do; her pony did, without second-guessing the outcome. Every day, as they walked down the country roads together, Star seemed to be able to sense when Steffy was going to ask her to trot. That little mare got ready to do so before Steffy ever gave her the command, as if she were finishing her thoughts for her.

They were becoming inseparable. The teenage cowgirl made it a point to never miss a day with her mare. She spent the next three weeks out at the barn with her, four hours a day, giving Star her hoof soaks and bleach-water therapy. Then she gave her a complete body massage. After that the two went jogging for miles up and down the country roads together. Star was dropping more weight and gaining more muscle mass every day. Steffy hardly noticed, though, since she was with her nonstop. She just wanted to get Star better as quickly as she could. The encouragement she'd received from Parry the last time he came out seemed to be all she needed to buckle down and keep the therapy going strong.

It was now near the end of October. Steffy stopped hosing Star off every day because it was getting a little cooler out. The chill of autumn was in the air. The leaves were changing color and falling to the ground. The crisp, cool air seemed to put both Steffy and Star into a peppier and somewhat feistier mood.

One day, while they were on one of their walks, Steffy decided to explore some woods. It was right before all the leaves had fallen, so she was able to discover a trail. The trees were so tall, and the changing color on all the leaves seemed to invite them right in. The sounds of the cars, trucks, and trains had disappeared. The only thing they could hear was the beautiful melody of birds singing and wings fluttering. Some birds flew in closer to get a better look at their new forest guests.

As the two walked, Steffy heard the sound of a stream getting closer and closer. Star heard it too, and the curious pony seemed eager to find it. They soon found the fast-moving water, and the frisky little pony arched her head and pawed at it. She splashed a little water on her girl. "Hey!

Watch it!" Steffy yelled. Then she gave Star a questioning grin and thought maybe her pony felt a little ornery. Perhaps her naughty, little mare had splashed her on purpose. Without missing a beat, Star pawed at the water again. Steffy got even wetter, proving her theory right.

"Oh yeah? I see how you are. Well, two can play at that game, little pony girl." Steffy said. The teenage redhead felt a little boisterous herself, so she kicked the water, splashing her pony right back. Star whinnied, hopped to the side, stepped all four hooves into the creek, and danced around. She playfully threw her head all about. Steffy found herself jumping into the creek too. The water was almost up to the top of her boots, but she hardly noticed. She was too busy mimicking her pony, who was stomping around and moving her head all over the place.

The two of them had the time of their lives while playing in that creek and acting like the crazy girls they were. They didn't stop playing until they were both exhausted. Then Steffy realized her feet were soaking in freezing water and becoming numb. She led her pony out of the creek and onto the other side. The carefree teenager thought about how the entire scenario would have looked if anyone had seen them, and then she laughed aloud. Star began whinnying as if she were laughing right along with her. This made Steffy laugh even harder.

The two of them managed to follow the trail out of the woods. It led them back to Currant Road, right where they needed to be. The giddy cowgirl was sure they must have left behind countless, confused wild animals. She decided the creatures must have thought their guests were slightly insane. In addition, she was convinced they were probably a bit relieved to see them go. The thought of that made her laugh even harder as they continued back to the barn, soaking wet, cold, and very happy. Steffy couldn't stop chuckling, though. In fact, she was still cracking up when they reached the edge of Mr. Holme's property.

Her face was in a lot of pain from smiling for so long. She feared the smile may remain permanent and that the pain in her abdomen may never subside. She wrapped one arm around Star and leaned onto her pony to rest herself. With the other hand, she held her belly. They finally walked into the barn. They stood there, so content and happy to just … be. They were as equally happy as the other. Steffy was almost sure she saw Star try to smile. She couldn't help but giggle some more, and her face and belly continued to hurt.

She put Star in her stall, and then the happy girl laid down on a bale of hay. She tried her best not to laugh anymore, for it was now too painful to do so. What a sight they were! Their days were filled with these kinds of explorations and playful silliness. Every day the two grew closer.

It was hard for Steffy to remember her life without her little mare. She tried to imagine what could have possibly been going on in her pony's mind. Star had gone from being a little orphaned pony, overweight and crippled, to being someone's pride and joy, getting pampered, and being loved like never before. It's fair to say that Star probably couldn't remember her life without Steffy either.

★ CHAPTER 13 ★

Out of the Danger Zone at Last

AFTER THREE MORE weeks of intense workouts and careful therapy, Parry was back to trim Star's hooves. He put all his tools next to her inside the barn, and he was surprised to see that little mare in such good shape. He chuckled as he spoke to Steffy. "Well, young lady, it looks as if this pony has lost a lot of unhealthy weight and gained some much-needed muscle. She is pretty fit." Then he patted Star's neck. "Her neck isn't thick anymore either." Then he patted her chest. "Look at the definition in her muscles."

After he examined all four hooves, he said, "The thrush is completely gone, and her abscesses are healing nicely. You are doing a great job, Steffy."

There was a long pause. Then she heard him say the magic words: "It looks like Star is out of the danger zone at last. Steffy, she is gonna make it!"

The first thing that Christian cowgirl did was look straight up to the heavens, and she gave a shout-out to God. "Thank You! Thank You! Thank You!" Then she gave Star a big hug. Finally, she thanked Parry sincerely for everything he had done for them.

"Now, you still won't ever be able to ride her," he said. "But you have a fine little mare here, and she is as cute as a button. *And* she is unbelievably well behaved, if I do say so myself." He let out another laugh.

"Well, I never expected to ever ride my mare. I only wanted to make her healthy again and get her on the road to recovery. I just wanted to be able to give her a second chance at life. And we did it,

Parry! She is gonna make it because we put her missing pieces back together again. Woo-hoo! Thank you! Thank you! Thank you!"

The two of them talked and laughed and smiled during the rest of the visit. The blacksmith trimmed Star's hooves, and then he wished Steffy an early happy birthday. He told her that her pony's hooves were looking so good that he wouldn't need to be out again for about five weeks. "It will be a little closer to Christmas when I need to be back to trim again. I hope that you and your family will have a very happy Thanksgiving. Looks like you have a lot to be thankful for," Parry said as he loaded his tools back into his truck. He instructed her to keep doing what she was doing with her pony. He told her she could go ahead and find a good vet for Star and get her an examination and vaccines.

Now that Star had improved this much, there would be no reason for a vet to feel the need for her to be put down. Star was at a healthy enough weight now. Her neck had thinned out, her hooves were looking more normal, the thrush was gone, and the abscesses were healing nicely. In addition, the pony's behavior had drastically improved. The two said goodbye.

The blacksmith left and Steffy stayed at the barn another half hour. She groomed her little mare and told her everything Parry had said. After that she decided to braid her mane. She made five braids along the side of Star's neck. Since Star's forelock was so thick, Steffy made only a little braid that lay on top of her bushy 1980s-style bangs. Steffy's little dumpling looked smashing. Once Steffy was satisfied with her adorable pony's "do," she hugged her tiny mare's neck and said in a ritzy accent, "Goodbye, gwaaageous. I will see you in the marrow, daaaaaahling." Then she giggled to herself, left the barn, hopped on her moped, and headed for home. The ecstatic teenager couldn't wait to get back home and tell her parents and sisters about Star and that she was definitely going to make it.

Once she got home, she was speaking nonstop while her whole family listened carefully to her. They were excited for her as they hung onto every word she said. They all knew how hard Steffy had been working to rehabilitate Star. They were the ones who had made it all possible for her to do it, with all the driving they had done up to this point, all the sacrifices they had made to keep those two together daily, and all the sacrifices they had seen Steffy make in her childhood. They witnessed the countless hours that their Steffer put into a pony that had appeared to be a lost cause. And now they saw that all her hard work hadn't been in vain. It had all paid off, every single last bit of it.

The animal Steffy had worked all those years for, the little sickly pony that had been at death's door, the mare God had chosen for her, had overcome some of her darkest moments and pulled through like a champ. Star was now healthy again. She was able to have a quality of life. She was able to be alive, happy, and loved.

After Steffy told her family all about this exciting news, she called her cousin Jason and told him about it too. He was so happy for her and Star. Meanwhile, his dad had bought him a pony at the local auction, and he had some incredible stories of his own to share with her. Jason told Steffy all about how he'd ridden his pony everywhere. Before and after school, the two had explored the countryside and discovered trails and new sights. His adventures were always exciting to hear. Steffy's favorites were the stories of how he and his pony would ride into town, down by the stores where everyone could see them. Oh, and her favorite story of all, best told by Jason's mom, was when she had called her son's friend's mom while looking for him. She asked, "Hi there. This is Jason's mom. Have you seen him anywhere?"

There was a long pause on the other end of the phone, and his friend's mom said slowly, "Um, yeah, he is here … and right now, he is riding a horse through my backyard as we speak."

Steffy and Jason loved the fact that they were not only cousins but also best of friends, and their love of horses solidified that bond. She was so happy for him. She didn't even think about what it would be like to be able to do the things he and his pony had done. It didn't even cross her mind how amazing it would be to ride Star, because the relationship she had with her pony and all the exploration and wonderful memories they were making on the ground were more than enough to make this girl happy. And now that she was sure Star would be with her for a very long time, she didn't think anything else could make her any happier.

After she and her cousin finished talking, Steffy called Debbie and asked her for the number to Doc Marty's office. His clinic was called "Western Veterinary Clinic." It was on Western Avenue in South

Bend. Debbie was happy to give her friend the information. She told Steffy, "Doc Marty is the best vet around. I wouldn't trust my animals to anyone else. You already know how amazing he is at teaching the Veterinary Science Club. That man is second to none! And he is gonna love that little mare of yours. How is Star doing anyway?"

Steffy was excited to fill her in on every single detail of Star's progress. She told her all about the extensive training and the therapy she was giving her pony. She told her about the weight Star had lost and the muscle tone she was developing. Debbie remained quiet and patient and she listened to everything her friend had to say. She was really glad to hear Star had improved and that she wouldn't have to be destroyed. It was a long shot, but Star had endured, and Steffy had never given up. They'd persevered and gotten through all the tough stuff, together.

"Well, kiddo, it looks like you did it," Debbie said. "I have to admit that I was a little scared for that mare of yours. She was in pretty bad shape. But you plugged away at it and brought her back around. You've become quite a good, little pony owner, Stef. Good job!"

Steffy was very happy to hear such nice compliments from Debbie. She knew her friend wouldn't have made them if she didn't mean them. They finished their conversation, and then Steffy called the Western Veterinary Clinic. She made Star's very first appointment with Doc Marty. She was so excited. Doc was able to be out at Star's barn the next day, and Steffy couldn't have been more thrilled. Doc Marty gave the excited teenager a hug upon arrival. And when he took a look at Star, he smiled from ear to ear and said, "Why, Steffy, she has to be *the* most *adorable* pony on the planet. Now where did you go and find this precious little cutie?"

Steffy took off at full speed with the entire story of how she'd worked five long years to get the grades needed to earn a pony. Then she continued, telling Doc Marty about how she'd found her little mare. The gentle vet gave Star a complete head-to-toe assessment as Steffy went on and on about their story. He just smiled and nodded. The horse-crazed teenager completed the story about the training and rehab, and then she stood there, trying to catch her breath. She was speaking so quickly and so loudly that she kept forgetting to breathe.

Doc Marty waited to make sure she was finished. Then he gave Star an injection of vaccines. Next, he de-wormed Star by inserting a tube into her nose that ran down her throat and into her stomach. Then he injected the medicine into it. Star seemed nervous, but she tolerated the procedure very well. She stood there like the well-trained pony she was. It helped a lot that Doc Marty was warm, friendly, and patient. The little pony could sense his kindness.

Doc Marty wasn't your typical vet. He cared about everybody. He loved Jesus with all his heart, mind, and strength. The way he cared for animals was truly a gift. And to be able to call him your pet's vet was truly an honor. Everyone who knew Doc Marty would agree. He was just that wonderful. Not only was Doc an inspiration, but his wife was an amazing person as well. She was a Proverbs 31 woman, who stood by him and helped him in every area of his life. She loved Jesus as well, and she was as affectionate as her husband. She helped Doc with the Veterinary Science Club kids, and everyone adored her.

The wonderful veterinarian patted Star on her neck. "This little pony was blessed. She was able to get you as her owner, and she is now healthy and happy. And you, young lady, deserve a medal for all the hard work and effort you put into her. God has big plans for you. You are determined and driven. Those are some very good qualities to have, young lady. I will see you two one month from today, same time, for Star's booster shots. If anything changes and you need to reschedule, just call my office and let them know. Until then, you two keep up the good work. And have fun. Those are doctor's orders!"

Doc Marty packed up his gear to leave. Then he turned around and said, "I am really proud of you, Steffy. You did very well!" Then he got into his truck, and Steffy waved as he drove away. She held onto Star's withers with her other hand. Her pony lowered her head to munch on the sweet, cool grass.

This Christian cowgirl sent a prayer up to heaven, thanking God for all they had accomplished together. God was to be praised. He knew the end from the beginning. He knew exactly what order all these events needed to be in to come to fruition. First, He had prepared Steffy for her pony and made sure she knew how to care for her. He'd made the young girl wait five whole years. Without that time, Steffy would have never obtained her own experiences and gained all the knowledge she'd acquired from studying up on equines. Her "horsey experiences" with all the horses she was able to ride were priceless adventures. They made her a better rider. They kept the hope alive in her heart, of someday owning her own pony.

And *then* God directed her to Missy, not to rent land from her but to find Star, the abandoned pony who needed Steffy every bit as much as Steffy needed her. Then God led Steffy to Parry, an educated horse trainer/blacksmith, who taught Steffy how to transform Star's life. And it was God who gave them the strength and the willpower to get through this crazy time. He brought Star into safety through the dedication of the Hacker family and Mr. Holme.

Steffy had so much to be thankful for. She didn't take any of it for granted either.

★ CHAPTER 14 ★

Steffy and Star's Miracle

I T BEGAN TO get colder, and all the leaves fell to the ground. Before they knew it, instead of jogging through colorful fallen leaves, Steffy and Star were treading through Northern Indiana's thick, white snow. Their routine was the same, however, but now Steffy wore her snowmobile suit and snow boots, and Star's coat was a thick, fuzzy atmosphere of warmth. The teenage cowgirl found herself snuggling up to her pony every chance she got to get a little warmer. Her four-hour-long visits seemed to drag on now that it was getting quite a bit colder. But not going to the barn wasn't an option.

Star still needed her exercise, and Steffy had to make sure there were no signs of any abscesses before she could stop soaking Star's hooves. Parry would be back out to the barn to address the issue, and Steffy's goal was to have Star's hooves completely abscess free by his next visit. She now had four weeks to work on therapy. The teenage cowgirl increased the amount of salt and soaked Star's hooves for an extra ten to twenty minutes each. It was too cold and snowy for Steffy to ride her moped out to the barn, so her family began taking turns again, dropping her off and picking her up. No one ever complained, though. They were all very happy to do it. Star was a big part of the family now, and everyone involved accepted that fact. Besides, that little pony was just too stinking cute to turn down. She was like a big, hairy dog with hooves. Steffy's parents and sisters adored her almost as much as she did.

There were times when Mr. Holme wasn't able to help, and Steffy's mom had to boil the water at home. She put it in thermoses and hauled it to the barn with her daughter. One night Steffy decided to do it herself and pour the boiling water into the thermoses, so her mom wouldn't have the burden of doing it. She managed to fill the first two containers without difficulty. But as she was pouring the last pan of water into the last thermos, she missed the opening. Approximately one quart of boiling hot water landed smack-dap on top of her bare foot. She screamed in pain, and her mom ran into the kitchen to see what had happened. Her daughter stood there, teary eyed, still holding the hot empty pan in one hand with her right foot up off the wet floor.

Sharon immediately helped Steffy up onto the counter, and then she ran cold water into the sink. She immersed her daughter's entire foot in the water. Steffy was crying at this point, and her mom wished so badly that she could have taken her daughter's place. She would have done so in a minute.

Sharon grabbed the first-aid kit. After carefully drying off Steffy's foot, she gently applied burn cream to the affected area, and then she wrapped the foot in gauze.

Steffy explained that she still had to go to the barn for Star's therapy. Her dad was now at her side, cleaning up the water on the floor. Her parents both tried desperately to talk her out of it. "Look, Steffer," her dad said, "I know you really want to get out to the barn to help your pony, but right now *you* need help!"

Her mom nodded in agreement. "Right now we need to focus on tending to *your* foot. You can worry about Star's hooves tomorrow, young lady."

Steffy tried to get her parents to understand that she really *needed* to soak her pony's hooves. She told them she'd increased the amount of salt and the length of time she was going to spend soaking them. Then she said, "Dad … Mom … Star needs me right now … just like I need you right now. Could you both go with me to the barn tonight and stay there and help me help her? I only have to stay long enough to soak her hooves. I won't do anything else but that. I promise. Just please help me. I don't want to take any chances of her getting worse. I don't want to risk a setback. It is so important to Star's health for me to be consistent with her therapy."

Her parents looked at each other, then at her. There were tear marks streaking down their daughter's freckled cheeks. Her eyes were somewhat swollen and bloodshot from crying. Her foot was bandaged up, and she looked pitiful. To her surprise, she managed to get both of her parents to agree to take her to her pony. They just couldn't say no to their little girl.

Tim said, "Okay, Steffer, your mom and I will take you and help you help Star. In fact, by the looks of things here, I imagine we will need to do this until your foot is well enough for you to walk on it. It may be a week or so till you can be dropped off to care for her alone."

Steffy's dad helped her up off the counter, and Sharon dressed her warmly. Then she put a fuzzy slipper on her daughter's injured foot. After that her mom gave her a couple of pain relievers and a glass of water. Then they all took the boiling water to the barn.

After helping Steffy through the snow and into the barn, they both followed her instructions and began soaking Star's hooves. It took half the time, since both of her parents were helping. Steffy's mom had her daughter sit on a bale of hay with her injured foot propped up on another bale as she and her husband completed Star's therapy. Her parents were impressed that their daughter had been doing this therapy for the past several months all by herself.

"So this is what you have been doing out here all this time? This is hard work, honey," her mom said.

"Yep, and while her hooves are soaking, I usually give her a full-body massage too. Then we jog along the road for a couple of hours and come back here to work on commands out in the paddock. And of course, I lunge her, muck her stall out, and feed her. That's why I need to be out here four hours every day."

"Well, I had no idea, Steffer," her dad said. "You have been doing a lot. I guess I just never gave much thought to what was going on out here. I sure am glad your mom and I had the chance to help you tonight."

Steffy smiled at her dad and said, "Me too."

Her mom added, "And we will help you tomorrow and the next night and every night after that. We will help you until that foot of yours is feeling better." Steffy smiled and thanked them both for everything.

Every day for two more weeks, her mom and dad boiled water, put it in thermoses, and took it and their daughter to the barn to soak her pony's hooves. They were out at the barn for only an hour each night. The neighbor who owned the palomino mucked all the stalls, including Star's, while Mr. Holme was away. When he came back from vacation, Mr. Holme resumed the responsibility of boiling Star's water every evening again.

In conclusion, Steffy was able to concentrate on getting her foot better. She had to walk on crutches for the first three days because her foot was too painful to put weight on it. After that, she walked with a limp. She didn't miss any school, though. Her grades were far too important. She had plenty of friends who helped carry her books to each class, so she was able to manage all right. On top of her foot was one giant blister that eventually burst and then healed. When it was healed completely, Steffy was able to lunge Star and walk her down the road, giving her proper exercise again. Star had gotten a little lazy, but Steffy was able to get her right back into the swing of things. She seemed to pick up where she had left off, and her little body toned right back up again.

Before she knew it, it was time for Parry to come out to trim Star's hooves again. Steffy told him about the hot water incident, and she even took her boot and sock off to show him the scar. She was kind of proud of it actually. Parry said, trying not to smile, "Chalk another one up for the injuries of a cowgirl." Then he looked her in the eye and gave her one of his famous half smiles. Then he said, "There are two kinds of cowgirls in this world ... those who have *been* hurt ..."

He let Steffy finish that sentence with, "And those who will *be* hurt." They both smiled at each other. Then Steffy put her sock and boot back on, and she told Parry about how her parents had agreed to soak her pony's hooves for her until her foot healed. He was pretty impressed with their willingness to help, and he asked her to thank them for him.

He arranged all his tools and inspected Star's hooves. After he trimmed them all down, he told her to come over and look at the bottom of each hoof. "Steffy, all her abscesses are gone. You have done very well."

Steffy smiled at him and said, "Really? That is so totally cool!" She ran her thumb across the bottom of each hoof and said, "The slits *are* gone, and the bottoms are smooth. That is *so* awesome! God is pretty cool, huh, Parry?"

The man just smiled back at her and nodded in agreement. The Christian cowgirl closed her eyes and immediately thanked God for healing her pony. Then she gave Star a kiss on the side of her fuzzy, little face.

After that Parry began looking the pony's legs over and feeling them carefully with his hands. Every now and again, he took a step back and scratched his head. Then he walked back over to her legs and rubbed them down again. Steffy watched his behavior and began to get concerned. Was something wrong?

Parry couldn't believe what he heard himself say. "Steffy," he said, "come here and tell me what you see." He pointed at Star's legs.

Steffy looked at where he was pointing and answered, "Um ... Star's legs?"

Then he motioned for her to walk over, and he had her run her hands down each one, starting from the top of each leg and going down to the hoof. "Steffy, what do you feel?" he asked her.

"Um ... I don't feel *anything*, Parry."

The blacksmith nodded. "That's right. You don't."

Now Steffy was completely confused, and she could only stand there and wonder what in the world his point might be.

He said, "You don't feel *anything* because her legs are not crooked anymore ... they are straight. I've never seen anything like it. They never should have been able to heal. Once tendons shrink and tighten, and bones grow crooked, they don't just heal up. Not like this."

Steffy stood there, waiting for him to say something else.

"Tell me again *exactly* what you have been doing these past four ... five months." He stood there and listened as Steffy explain about the hoof soaking and the bleach spray treatments she did every day. Then she said, "I give her a full-body massage from head to hoof, focusing mostly on her legs." She took a deep breath. "We take our walks. We jog most of the way. After that I usually lunge her in both directions for about ten to twenty minutes. Then I muck out her stall and feed and water her."

Parry stood there, listening to the young teenager, as he studied

Star's legs some more. Then he walked over and ran his hands down each leg one more time. After that he took a step back.

"What is it?" Steffy asked with concern. "Is Star all right?"

First, he looked at Steffy, then he looked at Star; then he looked back at Steffy again. Finally, he said, "She is more than all right, Steffy." He swallowed a lump that had been forming in the back of his throat. "I never thought I would ever say this to you, but ... Star's legs are straight. They are healed. Steffy ... you can ride her now."

The confused teenager looked at him and said, "*What?*"

Parry took a deep breath. "This is nothing short of a miracle. Star's legs are straight, and all her abscesses are gone, and ... you can ride her now."

That speechless cowgirl was literally starstruck (no pun intended). She had been chewing on a piece of hay and suddenly she stopped chewing, her jaw dropped, and that piece of hay just kind of fell out of her mouth. She stood there, completely limp. Her whole body grew a little weak, and she felt faint. She was choking on her words as they came out of her mouth. She managed to ask, "I can *ride* Star? I can *ride* my pony?"

Parry laughed. "Yep! You can start riding that little mare of yours anytime you want to."

The emotional teenager couldn't keep the tears from falling. She gently held Star's face in her hands and said, "We did it, girl. We didn't give up! We did it!" She kissed her fuzzy, little muzzle. Then she stood up quickly and began tapping her right hand on her leg nervously. She said over and over, to herself, "I don't have a bridle. I don't have a bridle."

Parry said, "Well, you don't have to ride her *right now*. Al-Bar has bridles. You can get one tomorrow and ride her then."

Steffy didn't even hear him. She was allowed to ride her pony, the same pony she'd been told would never be able to be ridden. All she could think about now was getting on Star's back and riding her.

She remembered that in the brush box Missy had given her, was a little pony-sized O-ring snaffle bit. Soon the wheels in her head started to turn. The ambitious teenager grabbed the pocket knife off the shelf. Then she found herself cutting the baling twine off the hay bales. Parry watched as she tied three strands of twine in a knot and closed Star's stall door on it. He continued observing her as she proceeded to braid the twine together. The young cowgirl took the braided twine and measured it from one corner of Star's mouth, up along her cheek bone, over her ears, and down the other side of her face to the other corner of her mouth. When she finished measuring, she cut the braided twine and tied it onto the snaffle bit. She looked her new bridle over. Then, using the same technique, she braided another three pieces of twine together. She tied them onto the bit as well, making one single contesting rein.

Once the homemade bridle was completed, she introduced it to the little mare. First, Steffy held the cold bit in her left hand to warm it up. Then, with her right hand, she held the top of the bridle and the rein. When Steffy thought the bit was warm enough, she put her left thumb into the left corner of Star's mouth and applied a little pressure. Her pony took the bit without much hesitation. Then Steffy slipped the top of the bridle over her mare's head and behind her ears. There she stood in the barn, with her pony wearing a homemade bridle made out of hay baling twine. The blacksmith just stood there in awe.

He watched the determined girl lead her pony out of the barn. There were approximately four to five inches of snow on the ground, and it was still falling. The scene was so beautiful. The snowflakes were exceptionally big, and there were so many. Parry began explaining to Steffy that Star hadn't been ridden in quite a long time. He told her Star may buck her off a few times. In short, he was trying to get it through to the little teenager that she should take it slow and that re-breaking a pony was serious work. He told her she needed to approach the situation with extreme caution. But Steffy didn't hear a word falling from his lips. All she could hear replaying in her mind was Parry saying, "You can ride Star now!"

She took Star to the middle of the paddock. Then she grabbed a handful of the Shetland's thick fluffy mane with her left hand and positioned her right hand on Star's back, near her withers. Without thinking of the consequences, she effortlessly jumped up, throwing her right leg over Star's body. Her bottom landed smack-dab onto the middle of her pony's back. As soon as the impact occurred, the confused pony gave two bucks, and then she jumped sideways.

Plop went Steffy on the ground. The fluffy white snow clouded up around her. Then it settled back down onto the paddock floor.

The young girl thought she might have heard Parry mumble something else as she jumped onto Star's back again. But she didn't make out what it was. He tried several more times to give Steffy instructions. However, the feisty little redhead proceeded to break Star her way, almost forgetting Parry was even there. Steffy was on Star this time for about three seconds before her pony reared up onto her hind legs. Her front legs were up off the ground, and her hooves pawed the air. They looked like the Lone Ranger and Silver.

Steffy grabbed a handful of Star's thick mane to keep from sliding off. The annoyed little pony didn't seem too happy about that, so she quickly began running and bucking in circles. They now looked like rodeo stars, and Parry could almost hear an eight-second buzzer sound as he watched Steffy fly through the air sideways. He cringed, slamming his eyes shut, as Steffy landed hard on the ground. She landed belly down, flat on her face.

That adrenaline-filled cowgirl lifted her face up out of the snow and picked herself up off the ground. She stomped her feet with every step as she approached her pony. Then, glaring fearlessly into her mare's eyes, she said in a stern and serious voice, with her teeth clenched, "I don't care if you buck me off all night long and I become one big bruise. I'm gonna ride you, and you're gonna let me."

The snow had melted off Steffy's round face. Parry couldn't see one freckle on it, for it was now as red as her hair. She was as serious as she had ever been. That girl was going to ride her pony if it took her all night.

Star bucked the determined redhead off two more times. Then she figured out that her girl wasn't going to give up. And that was when she finally stopped bucking.

Then, amazingly enough, Steffy found herself riding her pony. They were one unit with two heartbeats, trusting each other like never before. There were big, white snowflakes falling down all around them. It was a perfect scene.

To Steffy, it felt like a dream. She was sitting on her pony's back and *riding her*. It didn't seem real. It truly was nothing short of a miracle. It was Steffy and Star's miracle. And it *was* real. Steffy was riding Star, and they were walking off into the big pasture together, a trusting pony and her confident rider.

Being bareback and having not ridden in some time, Steffy seemed to lose her balance somewhat. She gripped her pony's belly with her legs, and Star started trotting. Steffy couldn't believe it. She was trotting on Star. It was so much fun.

Shortly into the trot, Steffy seemed to lose her balance a little more, so she squeezed her legs a bit harder to get a better grip, and Star began to canter. Steffy gathered a thick handful of Star's mane with her left hand as she controlled the rein with her right hand. Determined not to fall off, she centered herself on her pony's back.

Those two were soon effortlessly gliding across the pasture. The wind flew through Star's mane and lifted Steffy's long hair up off her shoulders. The snow hit their faces, and nothing had ever felt more perfect to either of them. They began to run faster and faster.

Parry finally motioned for Steffy to bring Star back to the barn. "Bring her on back. I don't want you to overdo it and risk Star's legs getting sore" Parry said. The teenager complied and headed back to the barn. As they were trotting back, Star noticed a pipe lying sideways on the ground. It was coming up out of the snow about six inches. One end of it rested on the fence. Steffy saw it too, but it was too late to avoid it, so she held onto Star's mane tightly with one hand while placing the rein on Star's neck with the other. Then she leaned forward as Star jumped over it. They flew over that pipe like they had been jumping together for years. Steffy had no problem holding on, and Parry was speechless as she rode up to him.

The teenage cowgirl stopped her mare and then slid off her back. After that she walked Star for a little bit to cool her off. Then her pony followed her right into the barn. Star stood there as her owner removed the homemade bridle from her face and applied her halter. She watched Steffy dip the bit into her water bucket to rinse it off.

Parry couldn't believe what he had just witnessed. He was literally unable to speak. He watched as Steffy put her pony in her stall and fed her. When he could finally begin to form words again, he said, "That was quite remarkable, young lady. I have never seen a fourteen-year-old do *that* before. You are exceptional. And I have to add, you are a natural."

Steffy smiled modestly in response.

"Well, now that Star is all good and broke, I am confident that you will both be getting a lot of riding time in. Just take it easy on your pony and yourself. Ride her a little and walk her a little. Let her get used to this riding business. You don't want to get her sore." Then he smiled as he saw tears of happiness running down Steffy's cheeks. He got a little choked up himself. He managed to say, "Congratulations, Steffy. You and Star did it!"

Steffy said, "Thank *you*, Parry! We couldn't have done any of this without you." Then she wiped her tears from her reddened cheeks with the back of her hand. "God brought you to us. He used you to teach me how to make Star better." Then she smiled at him sincerely.

"Merry Christmas, Steffy" was all he could manage to say. Then he fought back a tear, reached into Star's stall, and patted her neck. Then he grabbed his tools and walked out of the barn.

"Merry Christmas, Parry," Steffy said as she watched him leave. Her heart was so full of joy that she could hardly contain it. She couldn't believe what had just transpired. That girl couldn't just stand there. She wanted to shout from the rooftop what all God had done. She was pacing back and forth as Star munched on her hay. She still had about a half hour before someone would be there to pick her up.

Steffy had to tell someone. This was big news. This was huge. She'd actually *re-broke* and *rode* her pony, the same pony that never should have been ridden; the same pony that should have never even survived.

She looked around the barn and saw her notebook and pencil lying on the shelf. She grabbed them and jumped onto a couple of hay bales. Today was a day that would go down in history— "His" story, God's story. It was right then and there that she began to write down their roles in His story, the roles of a determined young girl and her courageous pony. By the grace of God, they'd beaten the odds and become an amazing team. She wrote down the story of *Starlite Mist: A New Beginning.*

★ THE ABC'S OF SALVATION ★

A: Admit you are a sinner (Romans 3:23).

B: Believe in Jesus (Acts 16:31).

C: Confess your sins (1 John 1:9).

★ A SAMPLE OF A SINNER'S PRAYER ★

Dear God, I admit that I am a sinner. The Bible says we are all sinners. I believe Jesus Christ is the Son of God. I believe He was born of the virgin Mary. I believe that Jesus died on the cross for my sins and rose again. And I believe He is now alive in heaven, preparing a place for me. I am so sorry for all my sins. Please forgive me for all of them. I promise to live for You from now on. I ask that Jesus will come live in my heart. And when I die, I will live with You forever and ever. Amen.

★ A NOTE FROM STEFANIE ★

Hi! If you made the decision to say this prayer and meant it with all your heart, then welcome to the Family of God! You are now saved. You are heaven bound.

Congratulations, you are a Christian or, as the Bible says, a disciple of Christ. When I first got saved, I was given some really good advice, and I would like to give that same advice to you:

First, find a good Bible-believing church and start going regularly. This step will help you to learn about God and His love for you.

Second, buy a Bible and read it every day. It is God's love letter to you. It will speak to you and help guide you through life.

Third, pray a lot. Praying is simply talking to God. The more you pray, the stronger your relationship with Him will be.

Whenever struggles come along and you find yourself feeling sad, remember, you will never be alone. God promises us that He will never leave us. He will be right by your side the whole time, always and forever and no matter what. No matter how bad things may seem, the Bible tells us that joy comes in the morning. The hard times never last forever. Give them some time; they will pass. Even if they seem unbearable, keep believing and keep hoping. Keep trusting in Him. God loves you so much. May He dearly bless you!

★ BOOKS BY STEFANIE JEAN SCOTT ★

★ P.S. ★

You can follow the author on: Facebook under "Stefanie Jean Scott" and also her website: starlitemist.com

If you or someone you know knew of this pony before or after she was rescued and would like to tell the author your story, please leave a detailed message for her on this Facebook page, or on her website. She would love to get any information that you might have.

If you are Parry, the blacksmith, the author would love to find you again and thank you. Yes, your name has been changed in the book, because the author would like to have your permission to use it. Unfortunately, she is unable to locate you. But she is still searching.

To every reader, I hope you were blessed by this story. I pray that each of you will always remember that:

"No matter what, you matter!" -Stefanie Jean Scott

★ GALLERY ★

Your Drawings Published!

Crystal J. Scott - age 26

Starlite Mist
Future Cover Photo

Starlite Mist
Was a Dream, Now a Reality

Star

Star says Hi
Neigh!